Hope in Grief

HOPE

IN

GRIEF

Addresses and Resources
for Christian Funerals

REUBEN C. BAERWALD, EDITOR

CONCORDIA PUBLISHING HOUSE · SAINT LOUIS

But we would not have you ignorant, brethren, concerning those who are asleep, that you may not grieve as others do who have no hope. For since we believe that Jesus died and rose again, even so, through Jesus, God will bring with Him those who have fallen asleep.

1 Thessalonians 4:13-14

Concordia Publishing House, St. Louis, Missouri

Concordia Publishing House Ltd., London, E. C. 1

© 1966 by Concordia Publishing House

Library of Congress Catalog Card No. 67-14950

MANUFACTURED IN THE UNITED STATES OF AMERICA

Contents

v

vi

PART I
Funerals and Worship

Funerals and Worship

A study of funeral customs concludes that "funeralization tends to be a reflection of the whole viewpoint, the *Weltanschauung,* the world outlook, the basic philosophy of life of the culture in which it is found. A cultural group buries its dead partly in keeping with its economic dimensions, partly in keeping with its outlooks." [1] The same study also indicates that American repsonses to death are very personal with ceremonial details determined by religious beliefs and details pertaining to the physical body left up to the funeral director, no general pattern prevailing.[2] Add to this the often made observation that the "life-oriented, future-oriented and youth-oriented style of American culture has made us particularly reluctant to look at death," [3] and you have the basis for the flurry of books and magazine articles on funerals, their cost and philosophy. The lack of a general pattern of response to death, the fear of being realistic about

---

[1] Robert W. Habenstein and William M. Lamers, *Funeral Customs the World Over* (Milwaukee: Bulfin Printers, Inc., 1960), p. 759.

[2] Ibid., p. 730.

[3] Russell J. Becker, "Funeral — Memorial or Burial?" *Pastoral Psychology,* XV (April 1964), 51.

death, inadequate and conflicting philosophies of life, and a materialistic culture have all contributed to the confusing debate over the theory and practice of American funerals.

Much of the criticism leveled at American funeral practices is aimed at the high cost of burial, the attempts at disguising death, customs developed from the untutored requests of emotionally upset and grief-stricken mourners, and well-meant attitudes of relatives and friends.

Various Views

There are those who believe that the purpose of a funeral is to show sympathy. The mourners are the center of attention. Every effort is made to respond to their grief with soothing words, soft music, poetry, and Scripture readings of an irenic nature. The simple presence of friends and relatives communicates sympathy and supports the grieving in their loneliness and sorrow.

Others believe that the funeral is an opportunity to pay one's last respects to the deceased. The center of attention is given to the dead. Attendance at the funeral indicates respect and honor for the person and life of the deceased. If there is a sermon, it is a eulogy citing achievements and memories. The civic and fraternal organizations add their rites celebrating the virtues of a valued member.

Certainly there is truth in the intention of these views even though they do not give great dimension to the concept of a funeral. Some aspects of both are present at most funerals. Several other views have much less to commend them. One such view seems to be that of a segment of undertakers who in the marketing of their wares emphasize the disguising of death. Elaborate embalming to present lifelike corpses, costly caskets of watertight construction with adjustable bed, a full array of slumber gowns, contrived lighting effects, elaborate floral settings, elegant slumber rooms, and a host of other costly possibilities are sold to take the sting away from death and to ease the pain of burial. Jessica Mitford cleverly brought such extravagances to public view in her now famous book, *The American Way of Death*.[4] Akin to this view is that of mourners who attempt to quiet their conscience or prove their love with elaborate funerals, providing a great show and costing far more than the responsible management of money would suggest.

Religious Dimension

One might charitably explain the absence of a more adequate religious dimension to our understanding of the funeral by pointing to the increasingly secular nature of American culture. But how shall we explain the disturbing realization that many churches add little or nothing to the meaning of burial? Frequently the crassest forms of our funeral customs are baptized and practiced

---

[4] Although the Mitford style quickly brought this book to national attention, a more careful and more penetrating treatment was published some years earlier, *The American Funeral: A Study in Guilt and Extravagance* (Washington, D. C.: Public Affairs Press, 1959), by Leroy Bowman. The Mitford volume has often been criticized for its generalizations, sensational examples, and a failure to give credit to the many funeral directors who are not involved in the practices the book describes.

in our parishes and, in fact, enjoy the status of hallowed tradition.

No doubt this is an example of a continuing threat to the Christian church as pointed out by Richard R. Caemmerer in his profound little volume, *The Church in the World*.[5] In it he indicates that the church must be aware of a world that has invaded her fellowship and undermines the uniqueness of her life and witness from the inside. A further explanation is found in Martin Marty's book, *The New Shape of American Religion*.[6] Marty argues that a powerful force in current American life is a fusion of vague theology, moralism, and patriotic sentiment which he calls "religion-in-general" and is espoused alike by many inside and outside the Christian church.

The Funeral Service

At least, one would expect the church to continue to make her distinctive contribution to the religious understanding of the funeral in the funeral sermon. Conflicting views also tend to emasculate this traditional form of teaching and witness. But some would argue that preaching is out of place in a burial service. The mourning family and relatives are too grief stricken for adequate participation. The friends who have come to the funeral are primarily interested in showing their sympathy and paying their respects to the deceased and have not come to be "preached at."

---

[5] Richard R. Caemmerer, *The Church in the World* (St. Louis: Concordia Publishing House, 1949).

[6] Martin E. Marty, *The New Shape of American Religion* (New York: Harper and Brothers, 1958).

Others believe that if the clergyman does anything beyond reading Scripture and prayer, he should limit himself to a few intimate words of sympathy as a friend and personal counselor of the family. Such a quiet and personal approach indicates the sympathetic understanding desired by the bereaved and gives the proper focus to the emotional needs of the mourners.

Another tradition considers the funeral service the last opportunity to present the record of achievement of the deceased and to provide public testimony of the high esteem in which the dead person was held by all.

Critical Review

Fortunately, the Christian church has her critics, and there are many signs that she is listening. Examples are easily multiplied. In 1954 the Church Social Relations Commission of Holy Trinity Episcopal Church at Oxford, Ohio, published a critical examination of the commercial aspects of funeral practices, the loss of "the historic depths of Christian meaning," the shift of burial services from the church to the funeral home, and the functioning of the funeral director as pastor and priest. The commission set up a recommended parish procedure for burials calling for a return to more specifically Christian customs and stating that "the burial service is a regular congregational service in the life of the church family. . . ." [7]

Similarly, Joseph E. McCabe devotes a chapter of his book, *The Power of God in a Parish Program,* to an eval-

---

[7] Reported in *Time,* LXIII (Jan. 18, 1954), 93—94.

uation of the Christian funeral.[8] He recalls how he went about preparing his congregation in suburban Philadelphia for more Christian, more helpful, and more reverent burial practices. His sermon, approved by the official board and mailed to the entire congregation, is a forceful call to funeral services in church, services which glorify God as well as comfort the bereaved, music which sounds a note of hope and victory, and other practices pointing to the theology involved in Christian burial.

Many have been alerting the church to the psychological needs of the mourners and the nature of grief, calling for reform in funeral practices to reflect these concerns. Paul E. Irion's book, *The Funeral and the Mourners,* and *Understanding Grief* by Edgar N. Jackson are helpful studies.

Efforts to restore the funeral sermon and to evaluate its content are also becoming more frequent. An example is an article, "The Funeral Sermon," by Michael Daves in *The Pulpit.*[9] Mr. Daves examines the weaknesses of the evangelistic sermon, the eulogy and the escapist type of preaching, and then points to more adequate content to meet the needs of the mourners.

Such criticisms merit careful attention. It is ironic that those services of the church which are most attended by the general public — weddings and funerals — have become least distinctive in their Christian witness. It is

---

[8] Joseph E. McCabe, *The Power of God in a Parish Program* (Philadelphia: The Westminster Press, 1959), pp. 73—84.

[9] Michael Daves, "The Funeral Sermon," *The Pulpit,* XXXV (September 1964), 258—59.

precisely these services which ought to clearly demonstrate the theology and hope of the Christian community
because of their "public" nature.

Reforms are long overdue. They are needed particularly in the concept of the funeral service itself, in some
of the funeral customs hallowed only by usage rather
than godly purpose, and in music that is often without
character and in direct conflict with the purpose of a
Christian service of burial.

Funeral as Worship

It is necessary to consider these matters briefly because
their relationship to the funeral sermon is crucial. In the
Christian church the concept of worship is a central factor
in determining the nature of the funeral service and the
content of the sermon. This concept includes several
considerations.

In the first place, the funeral deals with an assembled
congregation rather than with a mourning family and
visiting friends. This is not to say that the presence of
the mourning family and the specific purpose of the
assembly is ignored. But it does say that all who attend
such a service — mourners, members of the parish, visiting friends, working associates — are attending a worship service of the parish and are worshipers rather than
spectators.

Some might question whether a worshiping community
is really present at many funerals in metropolitan com-
munities where attendance is limited, few members of
the officiating pastor's parish are actually present, and
the service is not held in the church. Certainly the number of actual parishioners may be small, and the setting

of a funeral home limits somewhat the form of worship. But the congregating of a number of Christians in one place for Christian burial implies at least a worshiping assembly rather than an assembly of spectators.

Second, the chief purpose of the funeral service — as of any worship service — is to glorify God. It is God who confronts man in death. It is God who speaks in the Word read and preached. It is God who has acted in Jesus Christ to remove the sting of death through redemption from the power of sin and the consequences of rebellion. It is God who offers in Jesus Christ forgiveness of sin, comfort, hope, and the promise of resurrection. It is God who has given the faith by which men live and the fellowship of the church in which men can bear one another's burdens and share grief. The funeral service does not direct attention primarily to the dead or to those mourning the dead, but rather to God who wants to speak to the event of death.

Here the traditional orders of service from the liturgical experience of the church are most helpful. They keep the focus on God and man in a sharp and accurate theological perspective. Although the appointed orders of worship such as Matins and Vespers were not specifically prepared for burial services, they are flexible and surprisingly adaptable to the task of speaking the Word of God to one another on such occasions.

Some Christian communions have adequate burial services which provide a rich worship experience. They will not need to press other forms into double duty.

Third, the funeral service calls the congregation to respond in faith, praise, joy, hope, courage, and obedience. Consequently, the assembled congregation sings hymns and prays and ponders together the meaning of life and death within the context of the Christian faith as the Word is read and preached. The singing of hymns provides an excellent opportunity for Christian witness and for a demonstration of fellowship with the mourners. Christian hymnody is a treasury of the church's response to God's activity. In these expressions of faith from all ages worshipers can point one another beyond the immediate sorrow and raise the note of confidence and hope amid despair.

Music in the Funeral Service

It is in this context that music for the funeral service is considered. All too often both organist and soloist are unprepared for the full dimension of their task in the Christian funeral service. They frequently have little music available beyond the somber and sad pieces which try to capture the sentiment of the occasion and provide a background for the grief of the mourner. In reality, the music of the Christian funeral service ought to sound forth the notes of joy, gladness and victory, of strength and hope in the risen Christ. This does not mean that wedding music might be interchangeable for funeral music, but the theme of Easter and the triumphant fellowship of the saints as seen in the hymns of the church seem more appropriate than some of the more depressing hymns and sentimental tunes usually considered fitting. A true ministry is given in music when the choir or soloist and the organist point the congregation and the mourners to the victory of the resurrection of our Lord Jesus Christ and to the strong trust of God's people in their heavenly Father. Such music reinforces and contributes to the purpose of the Christian funeral service instead of simply underscoring the sadness and grief of the moment.

Other Customs

Other customs that have crept into burial services, such as the open casket, the viewing of the body following the service, the filling of the chancel with floral bouquets, each in their own way contribute to a nullifying of the intent of the Christian burial service.

Memorial Service

In recent years the memorial service has been strongly suggested.[10] The body is buried quickly and simply, followed by the worship service later in the day or on another day, perhaps the next Sunday. This form of funeral service without the presence of the body seeks to eliminate the necessity of elaborate embalming procedures, costly caskets, large displays of flowers, and the focus of attention on the physical body.

While some may find this form of burial service useful, critics have pointed out the unnecessary severity of the solution and the value of the presence of the casket in facing the reality of death. Russell J. Becker thoughtfully examines a memorial service in "Funeral — Memorial or Burial?" in the April 1964 issue of *Pastoral Psychology*. He calls the memorial service a "bland alternative to Christian burial of the dead," pointing to the use of a funeral pall to cover the casket, the elimination

---

[10] See Ernest Morgan, *A Manual of Simple Burial* (Burnsville, N. C.: The Celo Press, 1964).

of the public viewing of the body, and a tasteful limiting of flowers as ways to meet some of the crass and offensive aspects of the American funeral. He summarizes his position by saying:

> In short, the emphasis upon the memorial service as the alternative to the garish practices of those who have a funeral service to sell commends itself to the religious community only because it reverses the extravagant trends of the funeral industry. It is hardly an alternative to Christian burial of the dead.[11]

Preaching, a Strong Tradition

The preaching of a funeral sermon at burial services is still a strong tradition in many churches. The pastor leads the worshiping congregation as well as the bereaved family to the comfort and strength of the Word of God. The place and purpose of the sermon is largely determined by the concept of worship already described.

For this reason both the eulogy and the "intimate words" do not seem adequate for the occasion. The eulogy seems out of place because in the burial service the deceased is brought before the altar as a sinful man who has been redeemed by the grace of God in Jesus Christ, who lived under the forgiveness of sins, and whose hope was in his Lord rather than in his own personal achievements or merits. Similarly, the suggestion that he limit himself to only a few intimate words in a funeral service does not describe the real task of the Christian minister at such a time. Intimate words indeed have a place between pastor and mourning family. But such per-

---

[11] Russell Becker, p. 52.

sonal words of comfort and sympathy which carry the
friendship and bond of years of association have already
been spoken in pastoral visits to the family and also perhaps in private devotional opportunities previous to the
public funeral service. In the public funeral service the
pastor speaks not only as a personal friend but more
importantly as a spokesman for God to the assembled
congregation bringing a message from God which is
relevant to the specific occasion for which the congregation has assembled.

The Task of the Sermon

The task of the funeral sermon might be described in
the following ways: 1) to bring the comfort of the Gospel
of Jesus Christ in a time of grief and despair, 2) to proclaim God's strength made perfect in human weakness
and His grace as sufficient for lives of continuing ministry,
3) to present Jesus Christ as the firstfruits of those who
have fallen asleep, the basis of our Christian hope, 4) to
witness publicly to the joy of the Christian faith and to
the victory of God in the life of one of His saints.

Preaching Themes

Such grand purposes of the sermon demand great
preaching themes. These themes are broadly sketched in
the Bible and ready at hand for every Christian. It is
the task of preaching to make these themes relevant at
the time of death.

One theme that stands out immediately is the resurrection of our Lord Jesus Christ. His victory over death
announced a new age in which life is a gift of God to all

believers. Even as God once gave life to man by a word, so He has in the new age given life to men through the Word. Not only did Christ bring life abundantly to men through the forgiveness of sins, but He is "the firstfruits of those who have fallen asleep. . . . For as in Adam all die, so also in Christ shall all be made alive" (1 Cor. 15:20, 22). "We too believe . . . that He who raised the Lord Jesus will raise us also with Jesus and bring us . . . into His presence." (2 Cor. 4:13-14)

A related theme is the victory of the Gospel of Jesus Christ as evidenced in a Christian death. The enemies of man, which the Scriptures list as sin, law, flesh, world, Satan, and death itself, have not succeeded in dislodging or defeating the power of God in a Christian person when he has by God's grace finished his life a believing disciple. (2 Tim. 1:12; John 10:28)

The Christian concept of history also provides a theme for funeral preaching. In a day when life seems without purpose and direction for many, also birth and death may seem without significance or purpose. The Christian Gospel declares that God is the Lord of history — also the history of a man's life. Neither time nor man's existence is a hopeless circle but a part of a straight line beginning at a cross and culminating in the day of His coming. We are not unknown or worthless. We are purchased with a price and for a purpose. Through Baptism a Christian becomes part of the body of Christ and shares Christ's mission of saving the world. Each Christian, then, lives out his own part of this grand design of God to recapture the world through Jesus Christ, and his life or death must be viewed in this perspective rather than in terms of our own needs and relationships.

Still another theme is the communion of saints. Tied together in the body of Christ by the forgiveness of sins through the washing of regeneration in Baptism, Christians of all ages form a living communion that cannot be broken by death. The physical parting of men does not nullify the fellowship of God's people. Likewise, the mutual responsibility of the communion of saints to share joys and sorrows finds in bereavement the opportunity to demonstrate the love and concern for one another which strengthens those cut down by the loss of a loved one.

The Christian congregation needs to hear also the theme of Romans 8, where Paul sings a majestic hymn to the greatness of God's love and mercy. No earthly circumstance — no grief, no sorrow, no tragedy, no loss — can separate us from the love of God in Christ Jesus. A mourning family and congregation need to know that God speaks in love and will continue to do so in the days that lie ahead, even though the ways of His speaking seem strange and painful. Simple obedience, acceptance of the reality, may be involved here. But it need not be blind, only courageous and trusting.

There is also the continuing task of life facing the bereaved. Death stops the normal routine momentarily. But the hours move on and subsequent days are given by the grace of God to continue those Christian tasks which are yet undone. The call of God must come in times like these to carry His people through grief on into newness of life and continued service. Mere stoic ability to accept sorrow is not the goal. Rather an ability to bear the will of God because His strength undergirds each moment of our days and because we see the importance

God has attached to our lives as individuals even apart from the relationships we establish. Paul says it better:

> But we have this treasure in earthen vessels, to show that the transcendent power belongs to God and not to us. We are afflicted in every way, but not crushed; perplexed, but not driven to despair; persecuted but not forsaken; struck down, but not destroyed; always carrying in the body the death of Jesus, so that the life of Jesus may also be manifested in our bodies. For while we live we are always being given up to death for Jesus' sake, so that the life of Jesus may be manifested in our mortal flesh. (2 Cor. 4:7-11)

Then death itself must be faced. Death is no small enemy. Death is the final great consequence of man's sinful rebellion. Death does remind every man of his human frailty and of his complicity in the great failure of God's creation. The bare reminder of man's sinfulness and its consequence needs to be a part of Christian burial. But the very greatness of the enemy makes the victory of the resurrection so much more triumphant. The power of sin to reach out into all succeeding generations to bring low into the grave every man born of woman demonstrates anew the tremendous power of God's forgiveness which brings life and frees man from the fear of death.

Finally, simple praise to God for His goodness which He has shown to man as Creator, Preserver, and Redeemer. Every man's life and every man's relationship to others calls forth reasons for praise to God and rejoicing over His goodness and His care. The Christian example of the dead is not to be neglected, nor is the testimony of the saints to be forgotten.

Preaching Texts

These are some of the great themes which have comforted and strengthened Christians for countless generations. They are heard not only at funerals but also in the Scripture readings used in the Christian church for regular worship. Indeed, in the readings of the church appointed to be read Sunday after Sunday are often the most neglected texts for funeral preaching. There is no need for hasty scurrying to books of funeral sermon texts when death occurs in a Christian parish. It could well be that the most natural and relevant word that could be spoken lies at hand in the lessons of the season of the church year governing the life of a congregation at the moment.

There are of course those special texts scattered throughout the Scripture which seem unusually appropriate and filled with power for times of death. Such texts can either be fitted into the proper season of the church year or can be used as desired and be related to the season of the year and to the occasion.

Such texts are found in the course of a pastor's reading and study of the Scriptures. Some of the finest do not immediately call attention to themselves as funeral texts by simply paging through the Bible. But in the course of private devotional reading of the Bible, theological study, the preparation of sermons and other talks, and general reading, the full impact of certain words of Scripture become clear and suggest themselves for particular occasions like funerals. A good beginning in the search for texts would be the careful reading of the Psalms, the Gospel of John, Romans, and 2 Corinthians.

The sermons included in this book are representative of parish preaching for funerals under various circumstances. The choice of these sermons does not indicate an attempt to identify the greatest preachers nor even to suggest that these sermons are all ideal models. The choice does indicate the serious attempt made at the time of death to make the Christian faith relevant, using the themes that seemed appropriate to each preacher. Some styles are quite informal, some lean heavily on the life of the deceased for illustration and edification; and some are more objective in tone. But all indicate a pastoral intent.

Some of the sermons are by well-known men; some are by men not as well known. Some depict preaching under difficult circumstances. All are serious efforts at speaking for God through a worshiping congregation on the matters of life and death.

PART II
Funeral Addresses

Glory for Gloom — A Splendor Yet to Come

Romans 8:18-25   Victor A. Constien

Today we face what seems to be a paradox. God, by His grace, has called us to be His own sons and daughters, and so we are. Yet we suffer. God assures us that He has redeemed, restored, and forgiven us, and so He has. In His Son, Jesus Christ, He has mercifully awarded us the kind of life that is indestructible. Yet we are easily hurt and so quick to worry. We grieve, become overanxious, feel our energies drain away and eventually die. How can we understand this?

Our sister in the faith was a child of God. But now she is dead. Together with her husband and children we, too, are sons and daughters of the heavenly Father. But now we mourn, suffer under the absence of a loved one, and smart at the prospect of an increasing loneliness in the days to come. She learned to handle the truth that she must die. Will we learn to handle the grief and loss that her death creates?

Paul, apostle of Jesus Christ, helps us. He Himself suffered. He saw Christians suffering and dying in the midst of prosperity and the so-called good life. He also sensed that a believer might collapse in the face of suffering if he did not boldly accept affliction as an inevitable ingredient in his Christian existence. In the midst of life we are in death. So when Paul wrote to the Christians at Rome he did not ignore the tension they felt, forget what seemed to be a paradox, and hope that nobody would ask him about it. Instead he courageously faced up to his own suffering and theirs. He wanted his readers to know what the people of God have in store for them: glory for gloom — a splendor yet to come.

God has set our future in glory. He has the remedy for man's present gloom. That splendor to come is the perfect salve for our suffering, the effective ointment for our disappointment. His help is our hope.

In the eighth chapter of his Letter to the Romans, Paul spelled out this realistic encouragement for believers:

> I consider that the sufferings of this present time are not worth comparing with the glory that is to be revealed to us. For the creation waits with eager longing for the revealing of the sons of God; for the creation was subjected to futility, not by its own will, but by the will of him who subjected it in hope; because the creation itself will be set free from its bondage to decay and obtain the glorious liberty of the children of God. We know that the whole creation has been groaning in travail together until now; and not only the creation but we ourselves, who have the firstfruits of the Spirit, groan inwardly as we wait for adoption as sons, the redemption of our bodies. For in this hope we were saved. Now hope that is seen is not hope. For who hopes for what he sees? But if we hope for what we do not see, we wait for it with patience. (Rom. 8:18-25)

Every death of a believer is a time for careful thinking. The thinking we mean is that which Paul suggests. He considered, weighed in the balances, and then announced his conclusion. So this very funeral service is a good time for this kind of Christian calculation. It's a good opportunity to place our suffering on one side of the balances. We must bear the tragedy of this apparently untimely death, the suffering of an uncertain future. There are also other troubles, infirmities, conflicts not so easily resolved, needs not so easily met. At first glance it appears that the scales are heavily weighted on this side. But now God's own hand places into the opposite balance the splendor and glory which He has prepared in Christ's finished redemption for all those who look for His appearing. And even before He empties His hand of the coming splendor, we discover that His gifts of glory far outweigh what we must suffer. The sufferings we now endure bear no comparison with the glory He has in store for us. Let us comfort one another with those words!

The glory yet to come is a visible glory. In Jesus Christ, His Son, God has made His glory appear. We can see it in the face of a Savior, godsent. The shepherds saw the glory in the heavens when the angels sang of the birth of God incarnate. The disciples saw it when Jesus fed the hungry, healed the sick, and raised the dead to life again. Peter, James, and John witnessed the splendor on the Mount of Transfiguration. The face of Jesus blazed like the sun, and His garments were bright as light. But the fullest glory is yet to be revealed. It will be brighter even than His resurrection and His ascension into heaven. With the full glory of all His holy angels, at the Last Day He will usher all who look for Him in faith into eternal splendor. Watch for that glory.

In time, here and now, we must suffer and die because we fall short of the glory of God. He created us in His image and glory for a perfect communion with Himself, but we do not live up to His plan for us. We are not satisfied to receive His glory as a gift. Instead we insist on making our own glory and ignoring His. We are not content with the image of His life for us. Instead we determine to make our own life, denying that our life is in Him. Now we have earned the only wage that our sin can pay: death and the loss of God's glory. If we have harbored any illusions about our ability to glorify ourselves, those illusions are dashed at every funeral service. We were not born with a seed of glory, only with the seed of death. Every funeral service testifies to the fact that that seed bears its inevitable fruit. By one man, Adam, sin entered this world. Death entered with sin. So death, not glory, has passed upon all men, for all of us have sinned.

Jesus Christ came from the Father as the Second Adam to restore us to glory. He substituted His forgiveness for our guilt. For our death He gave up His life, and now we have that life through faith in Him. His resurrection from the dead has become our life everlasting. As He is crowned with glory, our glory once again is made eternally secure; for what He achieves He achieves not for Himself but for us. "We see Jesus, who for a little while was made lower than the angels, crowned with glory and honor because of the suffering of death, so that by the grace of God He might taste death for everyone" (Heb. 2:9). At the same time Christ Jesus is our Glory and our Hope for glory, the glory yet to come.

The splendor yet to come will be revealed *to* us and *in* us. The brilliant victory of our Lord's appearance at the Last Day will reach out and enfold us and all believers. The glory of our Lord will catch up our sister and all the others who have fallen asleep in Christ. Drawing those who are still alive to Himself, Christ Jesus will join us to all the saints that He gathers with Him. It will be a day of happy reunion in the splendor of the Savior of the nations. In that twinkling of an eye God will not only share His glory with us; He will put that glory in us. We will receive and participate in the glory that comes from Him. Without any limits or restrictions we will possess the ample life of sons and daughters of God. Then we will know in full the warmth of our Lord's smile, the power of His touch, the joy of His presence. And we will appreciate and rejoice in the compassion with which He hears us and treats us as His own.

For now the whole world is a waiting room. All creation anticipates the splendor yet to come. The universe groans as it waits, but it waits with expectation: "For the creation waits with eager longing for the revealing of the sons of God. . . . We know that the whole creation has been groaning in travail together until now; and not only the creation but we ourselves, who have the firstfruits of the Spirit, groan inwardly as we wait for adoption as sons, the redemption of our bodies." Our own sighs and longings blend with the groans of agony and protest that rise from the world itself. Because of man's sin, the world cannot be what it wants to be, either. Forces designed to help things grow and produce are so upset by man's sin that in the confusion they kill and destroy. Rains rise to floods. Winds whip themselves into hurricanes. Grassy plains disappear in bowls of dust. The world cries out under its burden, longing for the time of splendor when all its forces will be used again to achieve the purposes of God.

The apostle Paul reminds us that the groans of the world issue from its being in birth pangs. They forecast a coming joy, and by the world's labor pains God teaches us to await eagerly that day when we shall be born into the full freedom of the sons of God. Our Lord will release our bodies from the pains and pinches that torment us. He will set our minds free from the fears and anxieties that paralyze us. He will rescue us from the apathy and hardness of heart that hinder our service to Him.

Did you ever let your attention be diverted away from an athletic contest for a moment — perhaps to get into conversation with a friend? Then suddenly you felt the crowd around you jump to its feet. What did you do? You jumped up too. You craned your neck to see the excitement. You didn't want to miss anything. The death of a loved one, a fellow believer, can be that kind of moment in which God recalls us from all our diversions to give attention again to the real excitement, the coming glory. The return of our Lord Jesus Christ, the splendor yet to be revealed, is the excitement that demands our attention. That's the day when our Lord Jesus Christ will raise up all who are in the graves. Those who have faithfully awaited His coming will meet Him in the air to enter together into the heavenly Father's presence. Right now, today, here, God is training us to be the kind of people who share with the universe its eager expectation, who stretch our necks and strain our eyes to catch the first glimpse of that day when God's sons will be revealed.

With this expectation of the coming glory God comforts us and makes it possible for us to endure. He gives us the lasting power we need when He promises that the day is near. He reminds us that our suffering is temporary, the

glory of our sonship eternal. He teaches us that our suffering has a purpose. By it He can focus our attention
again on Himself and the fact that He is our deliverer from
sin and death. That's where the excitement is — in Him
and His final rescue. So God stirs within us the glowing
fires of a hope in Christ. If He died for us and rose again
for us, will He not also nourish within us the faith that
clings to His forgiveness? If He suffered even to the separation of Himself from His Father to secure our salvation,
will He not also give us the power to outlast our sufferings
so that we may enjoy the fruits of all His labors for us? If
He has by His bitter agony won for us the coming glory,
will He not also in His steadfast love, day by day, give us
the energy to reach for that glory? Did He not become the
Son of man that we might be made sons of God, kept by
the power of God to the day of our salvation?

In Christ Jesus God makes the splendor yet to come
the splendor that is already here. The deceased knew that
present splendor from the day of her baptism. At each
Holy Meal, each Lord's Supper, God kept her in that
splendor, the glory of a forgiven child of God. Our Lord
Jesus Christ does this also for us. He is the answer to our
anguish of heart. He is the one who allays our fears with
the promise of His presence and quiets our conscience with
the assurance of His forgiveness. He is the one who leads
us into the valley of the shadow of death and out again, because He is the only one who has passed this way before.

If there are some people who insist on living their lives
without our Lord Jesus Christ, then they must make the
best of it. But what you and I are saying to each other
right now is that we cannot live without Him. He is the
only one to bring strength to our weakness, hope to our

despair, pardon to our guilt, life for death, and glory for gloom. From what God has told us in Holy Scriptures this is exactly what our Lord Jesus Christ is able to do. As many Christians have said before us, "We know of nobody whom we would rather have do it." The life we now live in the flesh we live by the faith of the Son of God, who loved us and gave Himself for us. In Him we are more than conquerors. He gives us the strong hope of a future glory. He promises the present splendor of a helping Savior. We know that we must suffer. But now we can accept it and know that our hope is sharpened by it. "For I consider that the sufferings of this present time are not worth comparing with the glory that is to be revealed to us."

A Time When Only God Can Speak

1 Corinthians 15:53-58   Alfred M. Buls

What does a person say when death comes? For many people this is a problem, even a rather embarrassing problem. You can express your sympathy, and it is appreciated. You can express your concern. You can shift the thought for a moment and say, "It might have been worse, you know," and then relate an incident that involved even greater sorrow. Yet, all these approaches hardly come face to face with the grief and sorrow, the aching heart of the mourner. When you cannot find words to speak, then turn to God and let Him speak. At the death of a Christian so many of the passages of Holy Scripture apply. That is exactly what we will do now. We cannot find words; this is a time when only God can speak.

We are mortal. We are perishable. At one time or another everyone will either talk or think about this fact of life. Somewhere at the end of life lies death also for us. We may not like to think about this. We may even resist bringing it out into the open. It is so morbid. This moment forcibly reminds us of the truth of this fact. This mortality or perishable nature shows up, however, even before death. We become ill. We grow old and with age are no longer what we once were. Even the 40-year-old man begins to realize that when he plays ball he is not as quick or agile or able to bend and stretch as before.

Our bodies are subject to deterioration. The search for
the "fountain of youth" will always remain the wish and
the dream of some people. "For there is no distinction,
since all have sinned and fall short of the glory of God"
(Rom. 3:22b-23). This is a universal verdict that rests
upon us; this is a time to recall these words and to apply
them. Modern medicine, a gift of God for which we should
continually praise Him, still cannot remove our mortality,
though it may relieve and lengthen life.

Perhaps in our sophistication we have tried too hard to
give death a false face. At any rate, it isn't an easy thing
— especially at a time of mourning — to speak candidly
of God's judgment upon man and of death. "Keep your
chin up; you know it could be worse." "Think of something else, and get your mind off your sorrow." God
never speaks like that. What God does do is to break
through with the ringing victory message that despite
everything that may try to convince us, we are not hopelessly and helplessly in the grip of some inevitable and
impossible fate. Our Lord spoke of the seed that is planted
and then decays in the ground only to rise again as a plant,
a beautiful flower, a head of wheat for harvest. "Our com-
monwealth is in heaven, and from it we await a Savior,
the Lord Jesus Christ, who will change our lowly body
to be like His glorious body, by the power which enables
Him even to subject all things to Himself" (Phil. 3:20-21).
Who among us can understand the fullness of this passage?
It is like a bottomless pool of clear water. Yet it can
speak to us clearly for our refreshment.

Christ Jesus put an end to death and judgment for all
those who trust in Him. Hear Him out: "Since therefore

the children share in flesh and blood, He Himself likewise partook of the same nature, that through death He might destroy him who has the power of death, that is, the devil, and deliver all those who through fear of death were subject to lifelong bondage" (Heb. 2:14-15). Christ Jesus "abolished death and brought life and immortality to light through the Gospel" (2 Tim. 1:10). "I came that they may have life and have it abundantly." (John 10:10)

Sometimes I think we would do well at a memorial service like this just to come together and speak to one another those great promises of God through Christ. Here is a positive assurance. Here is the promise and covenant of our God. Those who come to Christ live, and though mortality is still their lot now, it will be changed to immortality, to that life in which we shall not perish, nor face the bonds of death. Praise be to God that we can remember on this day the faith and confession and life of your loved one!

It is a helpless feeling that we cannot prevent death. Not even the best medical attention could prevent death when the assassin's bullet killed the president of our country. Actually, though, sad as the separation at death is, it is far worse if the end of life here leaves nothing but the judgment of God beyond. If death meant only the end of all things — the end of all existence — it would be sad; yet the consequences would not be so fearful. But the sting of death is sin, and the power of sin is the Law. The picture is that of a sting that kills with its poison. Try as we might, we cannot free ourselves from the demands of the Law which demands perfection. The worst possible scourge is to be infected with the idea that we are self-sufficient, able to get by on our own.

We can, however, defy death even in the midst of sorrow that is real with its tears. The sting of death has been removed. We still see sin and imperfection, and experience it ourselves. We may find it very real in the way we confront a time of grief and sorrow; but the sting of death has been removed forever. We have comfort and hope.

The prophet Isaiah said it, "He will swallow up death forever, and the Lord God will wipe away tears from all faces, and the reproach of His people will He take away from all the earth; for the Lord has spoken (Is. 25:8). St. Paul says it again in our text: "When the perishable puts on the imperishable and the mortal puts on immortality, then shall come to pass the saying that is written: "Death is swallowed up in victory. O death, where is thy victory? O death, where is thy sting? Thanks be to God who gives us the victory through our Lord Jesus Christ." Everything that can be said about the victory of the Lord Jesus Christ is also a personal victory for the Christian. We need to speak to one another about this victory more than we do. This final victory is a reality for your loved one. Eternal life was no hazy idea for her. She talked to me about it. She knew the hope of heaven. This was her life; and it becomes your comfort and your hope.

"Therefore my beloved brethren, be steadfast, immovable, always abounding in the work of the Lord." The New Testament often pictures life as a pilgrimage. We are moving on along the road of life. We are not permanent residents. We have an eternal goal. For those who have died the pilgrimage is ended. You and I move on. Here, too, the Lord has something to say. "Stand fast!"

Trials and sorrows and difficulties, sometimes completely unexplainable and seemingly so unbearable, tempt us to say: "It isn't true." The journey isn't easy and we ought not to pretend that it is. It becomes tiring. We falter. We struggle. Yet the Lord says, "Stand fast . . . always abounding in the work of the Lord." Place your life in Christ. Take your burdens to Him. Listen to His promises and await His call.

When someone dies, our attention is forcefully focused on this journey. To have someone go before us makes us all the more anxious to join him at the goal. To reach the destination we also walk the road that lies before. "Be steadfast." This is an individual thing to be sure, but it also calls us to help one another. "To all who received Him, who believed in His name, He gave power to become children of God" (John 1:12). Let us keep on saying this to one another.

"Be steadfast, knowing that in the Lord your labor is not in vain." This is our comfort when life seems hopeless, without purpose, and difficult. Let no one convince you that life has no real goal. Don't let anyone take away the assurance that there is hope and that God's promises are sure. We often make promises that we cannot keep even if we want to. It is not so with God. It was Jesus who gave the promise: "Because I live, you will live also." (John 14:19)

Somewhere I came across a story that aptly expresses our feelings. A little blind girl used to sit with her mother before the great picture window of their home. The mother sat there searching for words to describe for her daughter what she saw: in the spring the mother spoke of flowers, thundershowers, and rabbits and squirrels at play in the backyard. In the summer, she told her of the full life of the plants and fields, and in the fall, the falling leaves and the rolling clouds. When winter came, it brought the blanket of snow and the designs of frost on the window. This little girl had an operation on her eyes. When the bandages were removed, she could see. Her first exclamation was: "Mother why didn't you tell me that it was so beautiful?" All that her mother could say was: "My words just couldn't do it." The glories, the victory, the great promises of life in Jesus Christ are just that way. We keep on hearing them. We keep on telling them to one another. In the meantime, my beloved fellow disciples of the risen Lord, let us patiently await the day when all of this will be ours by sight.

Blessed Be the Name of the Lord

Job 1:21   Samuel J. Roth

In the early church, when the number of Christians was comparatively small and persecution was common, they used to call the death of a Christian his "birthday." That sounds strange to us, since we are used to celebrating our birthday on the anniversary of our entry into this world. And we usually do so with some degree of festivity.

But the early Christians knew what they were doing. They lived in the first glow of radiance of the Christian age. They were very conscious of the fact that physical death is the doorway to a greater life, the ultimate destiny that God desires for everyone. They knew that to die is to sleep for a moment and then to awaken to life in the presence of God.

So it is fitting to call the deathday of a Christian his "birthday." He enters into a new dimension of that life which knows no end. And so it is entirely proper for us to say that the day of this Christian's death became his birthday. While it proved to be a day of sadness for us, we can be sure that it was a day of rejoicing for him, as birthdays ought to be — and a day of festivity in heaven.

He did not choose that birthday, of course, any more than he chose the date of his entrance into this world. "The Lord gave, and the Lord has taken away." But still we come here to say, "Blessed be the name of the Lord."

As we turn to our Lord to give Him our worship, He

also gives to us His strength. Today, if only we will open
our hearts to His message, He will tell us how to accept
His decision that our loved one should be taken from
us now.

As Christians of the New Testament age, we know
the Lord of whom Job spoke as the Holy Trinity: Father, Son, and Holy Ghost. It was in the name of that
Lord that this person experienced still another birth, his
birth into the Holy Christian church at the time of his baptism. Now, as we say, "Blessed be the name of the Lord,"
God has something to tell us in each one of the three Persons of the Trinity. God the Father, God the Son, and
God the Holy Spirit speak to us in turn to give us comfort
for our sorrow, direction for our thinking, and strength
for our life tomorrow.

First, God the Father, the Lord, speaks to us and says:
"Accept My decision *trustingly*. Remember that I am
your Father, and trust in Me as children should. Realize
that all human life is in My hands and that I know in
My eternal wisdom when is the best time for a person to
live and when it is best for him to die."

In His eternal wisdom God spans the centuries. He is
from eternity to eternity. He knows what is in store for
us tomorrow and throughout our life and beyond. You
and I, on the other hand, are confined to that narrow
moment we call "now." God is not restricted in that way.
He can decide with perfect wisdom when to give and when
to take away.

But it is not simply in God's wisdom that we trust. It
is especially in His fatherly love. It is this that moves us

to place ourselves and our loved one confidently into His hands.

"He who did not spare His own Son but gave Him up for us all, will He not also give us all things with Him?" (Rom. 8:32). God has proved His love for us in so many ways. In love He sent His Son to be our Savior. In love He called us to faith in that Savior. And it is only from this God who first loved us that we can find the answers to our questions that begin with "Why?" — or peace for our troubled minds when the answers seem still to be far away.

It is enough to know that whenever God acts, He acts like a Father out of love, even when His hand seems heavy upon us. When He chastens, it is still an act of love; and He knows it will work out for good to those who love Him.

Second, God the Son says: "Accept My decision *gratefully*. Worship today in thanksgiving." Blessed be the name of the Lord!

Part of our reason for being here today is to give God thanks for the blessings He bestowed upon our loved one and upon us through him during his lifetime.

But when Christ says, "Accept My decision with thanksgiving," He has something even more important in mind. Every physical blessing pales into insignificance when compared with the tremendous gift He has given us through His suffering and death.

Think of it! He has won for us the forgiveness of our sins! He has opened heaven's door! He is our Savior, and that title means everything. It means everything, that is, when we realize the seriousness of our sin, the depth of our need, the utter helplessness in which we find ourselves by nature. You members of the family knew the meaning of helplessness as you stood by the bedside of your loved one these past days. You knew that there was nothing that you could do. This is exactly how we must see ourselves with regard to our salvation. We are helpless; there is nothing we can do.

But God has done something! He has acted. Jesus Christ took our sin upon Himself and paid for it with His own death. And then He rose again to declare His victory.

We can say today, "O death, where is thy victory? O death, where is thy sting?" The sting of death is sin — but that sin is paid for! The strength of sin is the Law — but that Law is fulfilled! "Thanks be to God who gives us the victory through our Lord Jesus Christ." (1 Cor. 15: 55-57)

As much as we regret to part with our loved one, we can be eternally grateful to know that he committed himself to Jesus Christ as his Savior. Our hearts can sing for joy, "Blessed be the name of the Lord!" because it is the same Savior whom we worship today.

Because He has won the victory, we do not have to sorrow as those who have no hope. We lay our loved one to rest this day "in the hope of the resurrection to eternal life through our Lord Jesus Christ." And this hope is not a wistful dream; it is a firm certainty, as real as the resurrection of Christ Himself.

Finally, God the Holy Spirit speaks to us and says: "Accept My decision *prayerfully*." That is to say, see in this happening a message for your own lives, and in all humility pray to God for His Holy Spirit so that you may grow daily in faith and love and hope.

We need that Spirit so desperately because a thousand voices seek to call us away from God, a thousand forces seek to chain our affection to this world, a thousand attractions seek to pull our eyes downward from heaven to earth and make us forget our eternal destiny. In the ancient prayer of the church which we shall speak again this Sunday when this death is announced to the congregation, we say: "Teach us to number our days, that we may apply our hearts unto wisdom and finally be saved."

We may feel the need to pray for many things today. But the prayer we need to pray above all is for God Himself to reach into our lives and transform us. We need to repent of our neglect of Him. We need to repent of our misuse of His mercy.

And this is the marvel of His love: He understands, and He forgives . . . and He comes. He comes into our lives and brings with Him the comfort and the strength we need for moments like this. He enables us to take up the chorus even with trembling lips: "Blessed be the name of the Lord!"

He has reminded us once again that He is the Lord of life and death. He is the Lord of *our* life and death too. In His service there is joy — not drudgery, boredom, unhappiness, but joy! And today we pray for His Spirit that we may serve Him gladly, that we may turn over our lives to Him in ever greater measure, to be His own, to live under Him in his kingdom, to serve Him in everlasting righteousness, innocence, and blessedness!

May the Lord — Father, Son, and Holy Spirit — speak

clearly to your hearts today. As Lord He gives; as Lord He takes away. May He move you to accept His decision with trust, with gratitude, and with fervent prayer. And may He enable you to lift your hearts and voices to sing, "Blessed be the name of the Lord!"

On the Death of a Lonely Man

2 Corinthians 6:9-10   Arnold H. Heumann

The blessed Martin Luther once said: "The summons of death comes to us all, and no one can die for another. Every one must fight his own battle with death by himself, alone. We can shout into another's ears, but every one must himself be prepared for the time of death, for I will not be with you then, nor you with me. Therefore every one must himself know and be armed with the chief things which concern a Christian."*

We have before us just such a Christian man, one who lived alone and fought his battle with death by himself, alone. It was typical of his life that he spent his last day, as most of his days, quite alone. Death came to him the same way, quietly and alone.

And yet, a wonderful paradox of our Christian faith tells us that he was not alone, neither in life nor in death. For when a man is in fellowship with his God through Jesus Christ, he is never friendless and alone. This is but one of a whole series of Christian paradoxes that Paul

---

* Sermon on Invocavit Sunday, March 9, 1522, Wittenberg; *Sermons, I,* ed. and trans. John W. Doberstein, ed. Helmut T. Lehmann, *Luther's Works,* American Edition, Vol. 51 (Philadelphia: Muhlenberg Press, 1959), p. 70.

expresses in the Second Letter to the Corinthians. We will speak of three of them:

> As unknown and yet well known.
> As dying, and behold we live.
> As sorrowful, yet always rejoicing.

Ever since early childhood the departed brother found himself to be one of the world's "unknowns." His father died when he was still very young, and his mother soon followed her husband. He knew the rudderless, institutional life of an orphanage. Indeed, most of his life was lived without the solace of a mother's love and the steadying influence of a father's firm but gentle hand. Those who would have wanted to provide the love and care that were needed found themselves financially unable to do so. So he grew up without knowing the firm ties of love in the closeness of a family circle. Although his friends were loyal, they were few in number.

Even of such a child and man as this, Paul could say that he was "unknown and yet well known." God sticks by a man closer than a brother, and He is there with His supporting love even when the love of a father and a mother fails through death or some other cause.

Loneliness has never been a foreign feeling to many of God's children. David spent many long hours of loneliness in his younger years, days of persecution when he was hunted by the soldiers of King Saul. Perhaps it was as David thought of those days that he wrote: "My father and my mother have forsaken me, but the Lord will take me up. . . . Wait for the Lord; be strong, and let your heart take courage; yea, wait for the Lord!" (Ps. 27: 10, 14)

David himself knew what this child of God also knew: "Father of the fatherless and Protector of widows is God in His holy habitation." (Ps. 68:5)

Also in the New Testament we find the Lord comforting His own with the assurance, "I will not leave you desolate" (John 14:18). Such comfort is given a child or any person who has been adopted by God Himself in Holy Baptism, as Paul tells us: "When the time had fully come, God sent forth His Son, born of woman, born under the Law . . . so that we might receive adoption as sons. . . . So through God you are no longer a slave but a son, and if a son, then an heir" (Gal. 4:4-5, 7). This adoption takes place in our baptism, Paul tells us, when we "put on Christ" and become "Christ's . . . Abraham's offspring, heirs according to promise" (Gal. 3:27, 29). What better claim to identity — to being somebody and to being known — can a man have than to be assured that he is a child of God? "See what love the Father has given us," John reminds us, "that we should be called children of God" (1 John 3:1). Because this child of God was claimed by God for His own in baptism, he was "unknown and yet well known."

Another paradox of which we are reminded today is that a Christian is "dying, and behold he lives." Paul had many a close brush with death. At the beginning of this letter he recalls how very recently he had been so "unbearably crushed" that he despaired of life itself. "Why, we felt that we had received the sentence of death, but that was to make us rely not on ourselves but on God, who raises the dead." (2 Cor. 1:9)

This reliance on God and the life He gives, even in the face of death, is possible because of the paradox of God's love. The very Son of God was forsaken by the Father that we might not be forsaken but be received into sonship with the Father. The Son was disowned that we might be reclaimed by the Father. The Son entered death that we who were once hopeless urchins might have hope of newness of life. And in this fellowship of sonship we find, as did John, that "we have passed out of death into life" (1 John 3:14). Literally, this means that we have changed our real place of residence. We live no longer in the shadowy haunts of the orphanage of death but now in the palace of life, the bright and sunlit halls of our heavenly Father.

The passing of this child of God, then, is not a complete surrender to death, because the grave must finally surrender his body to the risen Lord when He returns to summon it from the grave to Himself. So then, when his heart stopped beating, our brother began that long stride that will carry him across the threshold of death into eternal life with his Lord. We have the Lord's word for it that to hear His Word and to believe in the Father who sent Him is to have eternal life and that even the grave must one day give up our bodies "to the resurrection of life" (John 5:24, 28-29). We die, and behold we live. In Christ we live forever in the resurrection.

We children of God may sometimes feel lonely, but we are never quite alone. Christ is with us. He is our Immanuel, "God with us." And as we are never the final victims of death, so we are never completely robbed of the joy that Christ gives us. "You will be sorrowful," He promised His disciples, "but your sorrow will turn into joy. . . . I will see you again and your hearts will rejoice, and no one will take your joy from you" (John 16:20, 22).

All sorrow is only "momentary" when we find our joy in Christ. When the angel said to the shepherds: "I bring you good tidings of great joy," he may well have been aware that a short time later, in the same city of David, there was to be a great slaughter of the infants by Herod's soldiers in an attempt to destroy this child. Though we may see ourselves now as mourning the loss of a cousin, brother, or friend, God sees us as "sorrowful, yet always rejoicing." This is the kind of rejoicing that can smile through tears. It is an unutterable and exalted joy even when we face various trials (1 Peter 1:6-8). This kind of joy is possible for us now, because we can still rejoice in the promise of God's love: the hope of the resurrection and eternal life.

Our departed brother, though separated from family and alone through much of his life, has entered the "family circle" that no stroke of death can break. He is well known. Lord, banish our sorrow and fill our hearts with peace and joy now and in Thine eternal presence.

The Word of the Lord Abides Forever

1 Peter 1:24-25   James G. Manz

How beautiful and lovely is springtime or early summer!
The leaves on the trees give shade, and others fairly burst
with life from the earth. The flowers and the foliage have
beauty and fragrance that are natural — far superior to
anything artificial. Life is about us everywhere. The very
air invigorates and seems to cleanse us — if we can get
away from the fumes and smoke and smog of the city.
These are the days of which we dream during the long
cold winter. Vacation time refreshes us and gives a new
perspective on life and work. Is it any wonder that June
is the favorite month for weddings?

Yet summer doesn't last very long! There aren't many
places on earth where the weather is "perfect" most of the
time. Winter, with its bad weather, is either with us or
before us. All too soon the days turn colder, the leaves
fall, and the snow and sleet descend on surroundings
glazed with treacherous ice. For many the winter brings
with it danger and sickness and death.

God Himself speaks to us through the movements within
nature. He tells us of youth and old age, of life and death.
What happens in nature also happens to us. We live, and
we die. How many of us who are listening to this sermon
will be here on earth among the living 25 or 50 years
hence?

All of us are in the same basic position when it comes to life and death. "The years of our life are threescore and ten, or even by reason of strength fourscore; yet their span is but toil and trouble; they are soon gone, and we fly away" (Ps. 90:10). It is no wonder that some of the Old Testament wisdom literature seems to be cynical and down to earth: "Vanity of vanities, says the Preacher, vanity of vanities! All is vanity. . . . What has been is what will be, and what has been done is what will be done; and there is nothing new under the sun." (Eccl. 1:2, 9)

We prepare for life and work in our childhood and youth. The best years are the "working years." Then we begin to take it easy and, hopefully, have leisure for family and friends and for travel in retirement. But death comes for everyone — rich and poor, wise and simple, high and low, good and evil. Think of President John F. Kennedy! He lies in his grave in Arlington National Cemetery, cut down in the prime of life by an assassin's bullet. He should have lived and served for 20 or 30 years more, according to our way of thinking. Early or late even he whose potential seems great must die. The psalmist gives us hardheaded wisdom when he says: "Put not your trust in princes, in a son of man, in whom there is no help. When his breath departs he returns to his earth; on that very day his plans perish" (Ps. 146:3-4). Our text states truth which we observe in life: "All flesh is like grass and all its glory like the flower of grass. The grass withers, and the flower falls. . . ." (1 Peter 1:24)

Death may result from so-called natural causes. It may follow a longer or shorter period of illness, or it may strike suddenly through an accident or tragedy or crime. But it always comes! It overtakes all forms of life in nature, all the creatures of the earth. And how often we find growth stunted, creatures dwarfed or deformed, and life frustrated by pain even in its prime. "The creation was subjected to futility, not of its own will but by the will of Him who subjected it in hope. . . . We know that the whole creation has been groaning in travail together until now." (Rom. 8:20, 22)

Why is it like this on earth? Why do we have to gather on this sad occasion for a funeral? Why isn't life eternal? Why is there always so much sorrow and suffering?

Holy Scripture teaches that it was sin which brought suffering and death to mankind and to the world. It isn't too fashionable to speak of this in some circles today. Sin is not mentioned as frequently as in former years even in some churches. There is a contemporary emphasis on this world and all its works, concerns, and problems. This is good and necessary. Civil rights and earthly justice and peace are indeed legitimate and essential concerns for every Christian. We pray for these blessings, and we should work for them.

Yet an earthly point of view, no matter how sincere or prophetic it may be, never reaches the full dimensions of human need and potential. God "has put eternity into man's mind" (Eccl. 3:11). All normal people have a certain consciousness of sin. Man desires more love and peace than this world can offer!

The Bible is clear in speaking of sin and death. "The soul that sins shall die" (Ezek. 18:4). "The wages of sin is death" (Rom. 6:23). We all die since "we were by nature children of wrath, like the rest of mankind" (Eph. 2:3). How could anything be clearer, or more calculated to destroy pride and self-righteousness? It all goes back to our first parents, who broke God's command. "Therefore as sin came into the world through one man and death through sin, and so death spread to all men because all men sinned." (Rom. 5:12)

It is impossible to understand this philosophically and rationally. We cannot explain the origin of evil, nor can we say how it could arise in Satan when God originally created everything good and perfect. We can't give a satisfactory explanation why an almighty God permits evil to continue to plague and confuse man.

We can refuse to think deeply about these things. We can even deny that we are sinners, "miserable sinners," as we confess in church. We can do all this and more. Or we can turn away from all this dark and unpleasant concern with sin and evil and simply "affirm life" or "celebrate life" with all the joy we can muster.

Man can do anything! He can deny whatever displeases him, and he can turn away from any serious concern with God and religion and eternal truth. Yet he cannot escape death! Every obituary in the daily papers, every cemetery, every funeral home, even every church, reminds man of his fate and destiny. The psalmist speaks realistically: "Yea, he shall see that even the wise die, the fool and the stupid alike must perish and leave their wealth to others. . . . Man cannot abide in his pomp; he is like the beasts that perish. This is the fate of those who have foolish confidence, the end of those who are pleased with their portion. . . . Straight to the grave they descend, and their form shall waste away; Sheol shall be their home." (Ps. 49:10, 12-14). The New Testament sums it all up in a few words: "It is appointed for men to die once, and after that comes judgment." (Heb. 9:27)

How terrible it would be if this were the only message we could give you on this occasion!

It is good to recite the Apostles' Creed together at a Christian funeral! Note that in it we confess our belief in Jesus Christ, God's only-begotten Son, "who was conceived by the Holy Ghost, born of the Virgin Mary; suffered under Pontius Pilate, was crucified, dead, and buried." Here we approach the heart of the whole matter: Jesus Christ lived, and He also died.

Why did He die? Christ's death was certainly not what we would call "natural." Scripture nowhere reports that He was even ill. We know from the inspired record that Christ was crucified, probably at the age of 33 or 34. He was executed just like many others of His day.

The formal charge of the Jewish leaders was that He had committed blasphemy by claiming to be the Son of God. This didn't worry Pontius Pilate at all. He regarded it as a religious matter of concern only to the Jews. Pilate gave his personal judgment in a few words: "I find no crime in him" (John 18:38). He permitted his soldiers to crucify Christ in order to keep the favor of the Jews. Christ died because His own people, through their leaders, desired His death. All this is sober history. And it certainly gives no basis for what is often called anti-Semitism!

The real reason for Christ's death was the same as the cause of our death: sin. Holy Scripture makes it absolutely clear that Jesus Christ died because of sin. Sin always results in suffering and death. Sin killed Jesus Christ! Yet there is this great difference: It wasn't Christ's sin that killed Him. He had none. He was "without sin" (Heb. 4:15), the only perfect human being who ever lived. "It was fitting that we should have such a high priest, holy, blameless, unstained, separated from sinners, exalted above the heavens." (Heb. 7:26)

It was *our sin* that killed Christ. He took upon Himself the whole load of our sin, of the sin of the world, and He died for it. He died for us, for all. Isaiah prophesied that this would happen. "The Lord has laid on Him the iniquity of us all. . . . By oppression and judgment He was taken away; and as for His generation, who considered that He was cut off out of the land of the living, stricken for the transgression of my people? And they made His grave with the wicked and with a rich man in His death, although He had done no violence and there was no deceit in His mouth" (Is. 53:6, 8-9). John the Baptist tells us of the fulfillment of all this when he says concerning Jesus Christ: "Behold, the Lamb of God, who takes away the sin of the world" (John 1:29). Paul spells it out so beautifully: "For our sake He made Him to be sin who knew no sin, so that in Him we might become the righteousness of God." (2 Cor. 5:21)

Christ's story does not end with His death on Good Friday. Death and the grave could not hold Him. Scripture also teaches, as we confess in the creed, that on "the third day He rose again from the dead."

The resurrection of Jesus Christ gives us comfort and hope at a time like this. Were it not for this glorious truth, the most that any preacher could offer at a funeral would be heartfelt personal sympathy and the collective sentiments of the parish.

Christ's victory over death was confirmed on the third day with His physical resurrection, an actual historical act. He could say to His disciples: "Why are you troubled, and why do questionings rise in your hearts? See My hands

and My feet, that it is I myself; handle Me, and see, for
a spirit has not flesh and bones as you see that I have"
(Luke 24:38-39). What is more, Christ's conquest of
death endures. In Old Testament times Elijah and Elisha
had raised children from the dead. Christ Himself raised
the daughter of Jairus, the young man of Nain, and Lazarus. But in time all these again died.

Christ's resurrection meant that His body was raised
indeed, but it also involved His glorification, His ascension,
and His eternal reign. He now lives forevermore. He
"sitteth on the right hand of God the Father almighty."
Christ is the New Man, the Second Adam, the "Firstborn
from the dead" (Col. 1:18). He is the first in a whole
new order of life, the Victor over death in the fullest sense.
He is "seated at the right hand of the throne of the Majesty
in heaven." (Heb. 8:1)

> For the sheep the Lamb hath bled,
> Sinless in the sinners' stead.
> "Christ is risen," today we cry;
> Now He lives no more to die.
> *TLH* 191:2

This glorious truth has far more meaning than we usually associate with history and dogma. It is full of comfort and promise for every believer — even the believer
who has died. Christ said at the grave of Lazarus: "I am
the Resurrection and the Life; he who believes in Me,
though he die, yet shall he live, and whoever lives and
believes in Me shall never die" (John 11:25-26). This is
why there can be hope and joy even now at this funeral.
This is the basis for the real and solid comfort that I am
privileged to bring to you who mourn the loss of a beloved

relative and friend. Our fellow mortal did not just die. He died in Christ, the Conqueror of death and the Lord of life. Scripture assures us: " 'Blessed are the dead who die in the Lord henceforth.' 'Blessed indeed,' says the Spirit, 'that they may rest from their labors, for their deeds follow them!' " (Rev. 14:13). This is the only solution to the universal problem of suffering and death. "That Word is the good news which was preached to you." (1 Peter 1:25)

Nothing that man can give you or tell you brings comfort and a promise like this. No one can attain eternal life by his own works or thoughts or merits. This promise and assurance of eternal life with Christ is God's gift of grace to all who truly repent and believe and live in the Savior.

Thank God that your loved one knew and believed in Jesus Christ. He has now departed to be with his Lord, and Paul assures us that this state is "far better" than any that is possible here on earth. (Phil. 1:23)

Consider, finally, what this means to you who remain to live out your days on earth. What other explanation and solution have we for the misery and pain of life and death? Like Peter of old, we say: "Lord, to whom shall we go? You have the words of eternal life." (John 6:68)

The realism and truth of our text lies in the promise of the Gospel. True it remains that "All flesh is like grass, and all its glory like the flower of grass. The grass withers, and the flower falls, but the Word of the Lord abides forever." "If we live, we live to the Lord, and if we die, we die to the Lord; so then, whether we live or whether we die, we are the Lord's" (Rom. 14:8). Thank God that in Christ we have forgiveness and everlasting life. For the promise of life which comforts us in this loss of a loved one is the same Gospel that sustains us as we live and struggle day by day during our sojourn on earth.

Blessings from the Right Hand of the Father

Ephesians 4:8, 10   Herman F. Neunaber

God has called one of our brothers home. Last Sunday evening He sent His holy angels to his bedside to close his eyes in death and place him in the care of his heavenly Father till the day of the resurrection.

Our brother's homegoing brings sadness to our hearts. A beloved husband and father, a well-respected gentleman, a fine churchman, and a devout Christian, he was an inspiration and a source of strength to many people. His departure brings sadness to all who knew him.

In His wisdom the Lord of life and death causes even this sadness to be sanctified as we remember the homegoing of another. It is the homegoing of Jesus Christ, who now sits in power at the right hand of the Father. Paul speaks of it in Eph. 4:8, 10: "When He ascended on high, He led a host of captives, and He gave gifts to men. . . . He who descended is He who also ascended far above all the heavens, that He might fill all things."

The words of this text assure us that those who die in the Lord are eternally blessed. "When He ascended on high, He led a host of captives." In these simple words the apostle tells us that Christ has subdued all of man's enemies. All the captors of man are now the captives of Christ, His prisoners.

Through the fall of the first parents all men came under the rule of powerful enemies: sin, death, and him who had the power of both, the devil. These enemies no man was able to conquer. Against them man was helpless. Had God not taken pity on the work of His hands, all would have been lost.

But the Son of God undertook the work of rescuing man and freeing him for a life of service to God. "When the time had fully come," Paul tells us, "God sent forth His Son, born of a woman, born under the Law, to redeem those who were under the Law, so that we might receive adoption as sons." (Gal. 4:4-5)

As true man the Son of God went into battle against these enemies. Christ struggled with sin. It could not conquer Him; He won the battle. Sin was defeated. Then Christ entered battle against death and took the worst that it could offer, death itself. But He broke its bonds and on the third day came forth from the tomb. Death, too, He had conquered.

Christ's emergence as Victor meant that the enemies of man had been overcome. Man was now free — free to live a life of service to God. Only one thing remained. After defeating our enemies, the Champion must ascend the throne of divine majesty and be crowned with heavenly glory. In His hand the scepter of power must come to rest.

All this took place through the ascension of Jesus and His coming to sit at the right hand of the Father. In the ascension Christ not only held a public triumphal procession through the gates of heaven but also proclaimed Himself absolute Lord over sin and death and hell.

Christ's ascension, then, shows how eternally blessed are those who die in the Lord. Sin and death and hell now lie subdued at the feet of the believer. Should death want to frighten the believer and hell open its jaws, the believer can confidently say with Paul: " 'Death is swallowed up in victory.' 'O death, where is thy victory? O death, where is thy sting?' The sting of death is sin, and the power of sin is the Law. But thanks be to God, who gives us the victory through our Lord Jesus Christ." (1 Cor. 15:54-57)

Not only has our Lord "led a host of captives"; our text says that He also "gave gifts to men." These are the gifts bestowed by the Holy Spirit and communicated to us through Word and Sacrament: the forgiveness of sin, life, and salvation. These gifts are ours as the life and death and resurrection of Jesus Christ are brought to bear upon us and we take hold of Him by faith as our Lord and Savior.

For those who die in the Lord these gifts mean life in the Father's house, where there is no sorrow or pain or distress but only the fullness of joy and pleasure forevermore, the final fulfillment of God's great plan for man to worship and serve and enjoy his Creator.

Our brother knew his Savior. He had received the gifts that the ascended Lord offers through Word and Sacrament. Through regular worship in the assembly of believers he received nurture for his faith and responded joyfully to the grace of God. His life of witness and service made it abundantly clear who was his Lord in life even unto death.

Now our brother rests in the care of his Father, where no enemy can touch him. He is safe in the Father's house.

The ascension of our Lord also has much meaning for

us who remain. It assures us of our Lord's continual presence.

This is especially important to you whose family head is now gone. No longer are you able to go to him for help and guidance. You who have depended on him for many things will miss his counsel and support. But you will not be left alone; the ascension of Jesus assures you of God's continued care.

Paul says in the text: "He who descended is He who also ascended far above all the heavens, that He might fill all things." To be sure, there are some who believe that the ascended Christ is no longer with us. They regard the ascension of Jesus as an abrupt departure from the fellowship of Christians. They say He is with us only in spirit.

Look at the text. Paul tells us that Christ ascended not merely into the heavens but "far above all the heavens, that He might *fill all things.*" His ascent was not a retreat into the heavens so that they might wall Him off from us. The heavens have become His footstool. He now fills all things with His divine majesty and power and glory.

Granted, this is a mystery. It is one of those things we cannot comprehend or fathom but do accept in child-like faith on the basis of Scripture statements. And how important a mystery it is for us who remain. Christ has not withdrawn Himself from us; rather, He has come very close. We need not first go to Judea in search of Him; in Word and Sacrament He is now near us with His grace and help and protection. He is with us unceasingly by interceding, ruling, providing, and protecting, that the gates of hell may have no power over His believers.

As your gracious Savior He now lives to intercede for you and to extend to you His constant and full grace. For your sake all power in heaven and earth is given to Him. He will permit nothing to tear you from His hand. He will be your shield and protection till He has you among those whom He has delivered, who sing eternal hallelujahs to Him in the temple of heaven.

Praise His name, and thank Him for His grace. May He keep you unto that day when you shall join your husband and father to sing praises unto the Lamb in the midst of the throne.

The Day of Death

Ecclesiastes 7:1

Enno O. Gahl

"The day of death is better than the day of birth."
What an unusual line. At first thought you might imagine
that the words were written by someone who had experienced too many reversals in life and in a moment of
despair came to declare, "I'd rather be dead than alive."

But such was not the writer of Ecclesiastes. He was
King Solomon of Israel, a wise and intelligent man. Following in the footsteps of his father David, he led his people to great heights of wealth and power. Solomon was
a successful and brilliant man. His fame spread far and
wide. He faced life with confidence and with courage.
And yet in his studied appraisal of life and death, he
said, "The day of death is better than the day of birth."

Solomon was not alone in this appraisal. The apostle
Paul wrote: "For to me to live is Christ, and to die is
gain" (Phil. 1:21). And again, "My desire is to depart
and be with Christ, for that is far better" (v. 23). Likewise the apostle John: "Blessed are the dead who die in
the Lord henceforth" (Rev. 14:13). The early Christians often referred to the day of one's death as a birthday into a new and better life. Christians today sing the
familiar hymn:

> Asleep in Jesus! Blessed sleep,
> From which none ever wakes to weep;

> A calm and undisturbed repose,
> Unbroken by the last of foes.
>
> *TLH* 587:1

What makes this all the more remarkable is the attitude of unbelief about death. The unbeliever faces death with a great deal of uncertainty and fear. Voltaire, the French writer, is said to have told his wife the day of his death: "It is today, my dear, that I take a perilous leap." Robert Browning called death the "Grand Perhaps." Lord Byron, echoing his countryman, said:

> Oh, God, it is a fearful thing
> To see the human soul take wing.

On his deathbed Thomas Hobbes said: "Now I am about to take my last voyage — a great leap in the dark." There are also the familiar lines from Shakespeare's *Hamlet*:

> To die, to sleep —
> To sleep, perchance to dream, ay there's the rub,
> For in that sleep of death what dreams may come
> When we have shuffled off this mortal coil,
> Must give us pause; there's the respect
> That makes calamity of so long life.
>
> .   .   .   .
>
> Who would fardels bear,
> To grunt and sweat under a weary life,
> But that the dread of something after death,
> The undiscovered country, from whose bourn
> No traveller returns, puzzles the will,
> And makes us rather bear those ills we have,
> Than fly to others that we know not of?

Unbelievers shudder at the thought of death. The "we know not what, we know not where" of death fills them with fear and dread. In contrast, the men of Scripture shout forth a challenge to death and ask: " 'O death, where is thy victory? O death, where is thy sting?' . . . Thanks be to God, who gives us the victory through our Lord Jesus Christ" (1 Cor. 15:55, 57). "To die is gain." "The day of death is better than the day of birth."

But is it an empty hope? Is it wishful thinking? Indeed not! Solomon could say that the day of death is better than the day of birth because he was aware that death brings an end to all earthly suffering and sorrow. The prophets of God were not gloomy men. But they faced the realities of life and called this world a vale of tears. "Man that is born of a woman," said Job (14:1), "is of few days and full of trouble." In a brief commentary on his own life, Jacob said, "Few and evil have been the days of the years of my life" (Gen. 47:9). The wise preacher of Ecclesiastes wrote: "I have seen everything that is done under the sun; and behold, all is vanity and a striving after wind" (1:14). The apostle Paul preached that "through many tribulations we must enter the kingdom of God" (Acts 14:22). But don't misunderstand; life also has its joys. "In the world you have tribulation; but be of good cheer, I have overcome the world," Jesus assured His disciples (John 16:33). "Rejoice in the Lord always; again I will say, Rejoice," the apostle Paul encouraged (Phil. 4:4). But in a world of sin there is no perfect joy. The anxieties, the frustrations, the heartaches, the griefs, and the pains of life strike all.

This was true also of our departed brother. He was blessed with a wonderful family and a happy disposition. He could get a chuckle out of a youngster sloshing through a puddle of water. But in these last weeks and months

his strength was failing him. There were restless, sleep-
less nights and the gnawing pain of an incurable disease.
He prayed that the Lord would cut short his days of
suffering, and the Lord did just that through death. The
moment he breathed his last brought an end to all earthly
suffering and sorrow.

When Solomon asserted that the day of death is better
than the day of birth, he was confident that death is the
door to eternal life. Even as Jesus' life culminated not
only in a resurrection from the dead but also in a triumphant ascension into heaven, so He assures all who
trust in Him and follow Him: "Where I am you may be
also" (John 14:3). This is the heart of the Gospel. Jesus
Christ came into the world to save sinners. He laid down
His life on the cross that we might have life and salvation in His name. He has "purchased and won me from
all sins, from death, and from the power of the devil,
not with gold or silver but with His holy, precious blood
and with His innocent suffering and death, that I may be
His own and live under Him in His kingdom and serve
Him in everlasting righteousness, innocence, and blessedness." His resurrection from the dead is our guarantee
that the body here sown in corruption will rise again on
the Last Day to live eternally with God in heaven.

Let us comfort one another with this thought: "The
sufferings of this present time are not worth comparing
with the glory that is to be revealed to us" (Rom. 8:18).
Those before the throne of God "shall hunger no more,
neither thirst any more; the sun shall not strike them,
nor any scorching heat. . . . God will wipe away every
tear from their eyes." (Rev. 8:16-17)

Is it any wonder, then, that the apostle Paul could say that to die is gain, that John could write that the dead are blessed, or that Solomon drew the conclusion that "the day of death is better than the day of birth"? In Christ there is no enduring death. "I am the Resurrection and the Life; he who believes in Me, though he die, yet shall he live, and whoever lives and believes in Me shall never die" (John 11:25-26). Death is not a funeral march to the grave but a triumphant march to the throne of God. It is better than the day of one's birth.

In This You Rejoice

1 Peter 1:3-9   Alton F. Wedel

An English pastor tells the story of a memorable night in his minstry when he was called to a parish home where one of eight children lay dying of an incurable illness. It was apparent that the end was near for little Mary. The entire family had gathered in her room to be with her when the angels came.

After Mary's last breath, her father placed a tiny mirror to her lips, then stepped away and said in a quiet, broken voice, "Mary is with the Lord; let us sing a hymn of praise." And with that the whole family — mother, father, and all the children — sang with one heart and one voice, even through the tears that stained their cheeks:

> Praise God, from whom all blessings flow;
> Praise Him, all creatures here below;
> Praise Him above, ye heavenly host:
> Praise Father, Son, and Holy Ghost.

And the pastor tells us that beyond the song of praise that filled the deathroom it seemed he could hear the angels sing as they welcomed little Mary to the company of heaven.

Our Christian faith has in its heart a song that cannot be silenced, a praise that our tears cannot still. The great Lutheran hymn writer Paul Gerhardt went to the

cemetery six times — behind the caskets of his wife and
five children. But the greatest hymns of praise in our
hymnal come from the heart and pen of Gerhardt —
hymns like the Christmas anthem "All My Heart This
Night Rejoices"; the Easter triumph song "Awake, My
Heart, with Gladness"; or the hymn of comfort "Why
Should Cross and Trial Grieve Me?"

It is difficult for us to understand a song of praise in
time of grief. It is difficult for us to understand the death
that is the reason for our being here today; the loss that
we have now sustained; the long, hard days of anxious
care within these recent weeks; and the prospect of tomorrow's sorrow when we go back to walk alone where
once we walked with someone close to us. We have
grown calloused with the years toward death. We have
learned that no one can escape it, we expect the old to
die, and we realize the young may die. But death is always difficult to understand, no matter when it comes. It
is particularly difficult to understand when it seems to
take us out of turn.

We who gather here with you today are sensitive to
the sorrow and the anxious void and the disappointed
hopes with which we now are left. We do not attempt an
explanation; we confess we have no explanation. God's
ways are not our ways; His thoughts are not our thoughts.

But we do not need an explanation, nor do we look
for reasons. We need a cure — a cure to turn this tragedy
to triumph, our tears to antiphons of praise. And we
have that cure! This is a day of triumph! We can sing
a eulogy of praise to God, who has given us a living hope
in the resurrection of our Lord, an inheritance that cannot

perish, a life that never ends, a reason for rejoicing even in our sadness.

> Blessed be the God and Father of our Lord Jesus Christ! By His great mercy we have been born anew to a living hope through the resurrection of Jesus Christ from the dead, and to an inheritance which is imperishable, undefiled, and unfading. . . . In this you rejoice.

Do you get the message? The apostle Peter, when he wrote this chapter of the Word, wanted us to understand that something great had happened — something that had changed the dismal death march of humanity into a triumphant victory march to life. He wanted us to understand in moments just like these that our tragedy is not the tragedy we think it is, that our loss is gain, our death is life. He wanted us to share with him the relief and joy he knew when, after examining the opened tomb of Jesus with wonder, he learned from the women of the angels' victory cry, "He is not here; He is risen!"

There had been a time when Peter — the rest of the disciples too — knew the kind of grief that breaks our hearts today. The Savior whom he had seen, believed, and loved had died the death of Calvary, and Peter's hopes were crushed, his faith shattered. What would he do now? Death had put a period to whatever mission Jesus may have had as it seemed to cut Him down in the midst of His career. And death had put a period behind whatever hopes the disciples may have had in following Him. But it has always been like that. The sons of men are born, they live awhile, and they die. We spend our years as a tale that is told, and when it is told there is nothing left but the memory and the disappointed hopes in the defeat of death. There is an obituary column back in the Book of Genesis — you will find it in the fifth chapter — that records the lives of 10 generations of the sons of Adam. It tells us that these men were born, that they lived their span of years, that they had sons and daughters, and then the curtain falls on each with three simple words, "and he died." It sounds so futile, so final, so tragic. Is there no end to it? Do we still die the common death of all men? Is this the end — of life, of hope?

> Blessed be the God and Father of our Lord Jesus Christ. By His great mercy we have been born anew to a living hope through the resurrection of Jesus Christ from the dead.

Jesus did not take *His* place in the death march of man; He took *our* place. He did not continue the march; He brought an end to it. He died for all, and in the power of His resurrection He abolished death and brought life and immortality to light.

It is important that we understand this, not only to share the joy of Peter in the new and living hope that the resurrection of the Christ has given us but also to rejoice today in the triumph of the Savior that transformed this death to life. Christ died for us, and when He died He met head on the power of sin and Satan that seeks our life's destruction. Hell hurled the power of death at Him as He bore our sins in His own body, but the greatest power that hell could hurl could not contain Him. He broke the grip of death, rolled back the gravestone, and secured the victory. The guilt of sin that must condemn a man to death has been removed; the barriers are broken down. Death is no longer death; it is the bridge to life eternal. Its power has been broken, its terror torn away, its sting removed. Death is the changing of the scenes from this life to the next, from earth to heaven. Christ's resurrection is the guarantee of ours.

So there is hope — certain hope. We no longer mark the passing of the years with wistful sighs and wishes that something still might happen to delay our dying; we know that something has already happened to abolish death. We do not look forward with uncertain hope that we might live to see our dreams fulfilled and work accomplished. Our hope is sealed and certain! We have an inheritance in heaven reserved for us — it has our name on it. We are not at prayer today to mark the end of life, but to praise the God who by His mercy has received a loved one to Himself at home and brought him to the end and goal of faith: the salvation of his soul. There were times within these recent weeks when things looked hopeful, when it seemed there still might be a chance for his recovery, and when you prayed for miracles. Let me tell you that as surely as Christ is risen from the dead your prayers have now been answered. The miracle of life has been wrought. Recovery has been complete. This is the glory of the resurrection Gospel that where the earthly outlook is dimmest, the heavenly hope is brightest, and where the defeat is most final, the victory is most glorious.

In this you rejoice! This is a day of triumph, and even through the heartbreak, even through the grief of separation weighing like a heavy burden on our hearts, we sing our triumph song.

In this you rejoice, though now for a little while you may have to suffer various trials, so that the genuineness of your faith, more precious than gold which though perishable is tested by fire, may redound to praise and glory and honor at the revelation of Jesus Christ.

You rejoice today in the miracle of mercy that gave ————— new birth to a living hope through the resurrection of the Christ. The confession of his helplessness as with folded hands he went with us before the throne of God in prayer, the confession of his sins as he received the Holy Sacrament, and the confession of his faith as we commended him into the gracious hands of Jesus — these are the tokens of the Spirit's witness that he is a child of God by faith. In this you now rejoice.

You rejoice today in the promises of mercy the Christ has given us, promises that He has sealed and guaranteed with His own resurrection from the dead. "In My Father's house are many mansions. . . . I go to prepare a place for you" (John 14:2). "Because I live, you will live also" (14:19). "I am the Resurrection and the Life; he who believes in Me, though he die, yet shall he live, and whoever lives and believes in Me shall never die" (11:25-26). In this you now rejoice.

You rejoice today in the miracle of mercy that we, too, have been born anew to a living hope through the resurrection of Jesus Christ from the dead. "Without having seen Him you love Him; though you do not now see Him, you believe in Him and rejoice with unutterable and exalted joy." This is — we underscore it — a miracle of grace, for only by His mercy has the Spirit given us the faith to see beyond the earth's horizon to the inheritance of everlasting life where we, like our loved one, will be forever with the Lord. In this you now rejoice.

And you rejoice today in the power of the mercy that throws a guard around you to keep you in the salvation that is ready to be revealed in the last time. As children of the heavenly Father, we are not the hapless victims of circumstance. Our living hope, secured by Jesus' resurrection, is that our sins have been forgiven and that our hand is in the hand of God. If today we affirm that our loved one is with Jesus, we may as certainly affirm that the Lord is here with us. His treasured word, "I will never fail you nor forsake you" (Heb. 13:5), is especially treasured now. In this you now rejoice.

Our faith is founded on the victory of Jesus over death. Our faith is fortified by the power of God, who gave it. Our faith is fulfilled in the goal of life to which He brings us in the day of His appearing. In this we now rejoice. Our song of praise cannot be stilled.

In the Name of Jesus

John 11:20-27   Adalbert R. Kretzmann

We come back to the Bethany home. We have been there before. Then everything seemed tranquil and happy, for Mary and Martha had no difficulty more acute than choosing between the good things and the lesser things. But now the home of Mary and Martha and Lazarus is in a time of deep trouble. We prefer to think of them as a *happy family,* a family that is happy because the love of God is in their midst and is respected, understood, and cherished. We dread the day when tribulation comes and makes of them an *anxious family,* as when Lazarus is sick and the doctors can no longer help. But when somehow or other the idea got through that the sisters would soon be alone, when they trembled at the prospect of being without the brother whom they loved, they sent an urgent message to Jesus: "Lord, he whom You love is ill." (John 11:3)

Then in the course of things they became a *bereaved family,* a family laboring to accept the fact that Lazarus is dead while assuming that our Lord, in spite of their plea, had apparently decided that this would be a good thing and that Lazarus should go to his rest. Soon there comes the marvel of faith; the family that had been happy, then grew anxious and bereaved, suddenly regained its happiness and filled with gratitude because the Voice commanded, "Lazarus, come forth!" To be sure, the recovery cycle in our own lives is seldom so smooth and easy. But this eleventh chapter of John is, as Luther says, an excellent bridge to the Passiontide and to our resurrection hope. Unless we enter the Passiontide absolutely sure that "You are the Christ, the Son of God," we will always be in doubt about what is happening there; we will wonder whether He will come off second best who stands on trial before Caiaphas and Annas and Pilate and Herod; we will wonder about the outcome when the mob begins to shout, "His blood be on us and on our children."

Once you know who He is, you can watch with a calm objectivity while still feeling yourselves involved and confident in the knowledge that "Jesus Christ is Lord," "Lord of life and death," "Lord of lords and King of kings." Perhaps this is what Martha meant — that God had reached down into the history of man and had made Himself manifest, had revealed Himself in Jesus Christ as Lord.

The Lord is interested in the great issues of life and death. Martha says it: "Lord, if You had been here, this would not have happened." So often we are sure that He is not there and that things are happening without His will, that somehow someone has derailed the power of God or shortened His arm or blocked Him out or something has happened. He is not there. "Lord, if You had been here." But from this lesson you see that the friends of Jesus had strange things to learn. The first is that they are not exempt from suffering. With the whole clan, with all their sons and daughters in affliction over all the world, they will also come in for their share of suffering. Not only others but also they will shed their tears and cling to their loved ones in vain. There will be no answer but that God makes no mistakes. The friends of Jesus must also discover that in their suffering they can turn directly to Him. They need not go through any intermediary. They need not have a pastor to do the praying for them, saints to intercede for them, or Mary to make the final appeal. They can go directly to Him! Then they will learn that sometimes the response of our Lord, though still in grace and mercy, comes in such a way it seems to aggravate the evil.

Why does He wait so long? Why does He prolong the agony of our loved ones? Why does He not heal those who are afflicted with incurable diseases? Otherwise, why does He not take them home at once?

I think He wants us all to learn, as His family, that we have a happy issue out of all our suffering. Somehow out of all this He brings us a great new thing. This is what we have to learn here and now. We tell ourselves over and over that life is a battle. But only when we come face to face with Jesus do we realize that the battle has an end, that through death it rises to a victory, and that the apostles go singing across the ancient world: "Thanks be to God, who gives us the victory through our Lord Jesus Christ." Otherwise we have no triumphs at the end of our days. We get weaker and weaker, and the sickness grows more grievous and our helplessness more complete. It is only through death that the victory is there and we become "more than conquerors through Him who loved us."

Life is hope. We keep on hoping for some new thing, for some great thing, for some good thing, and it never happens. Then comes death and we, who were the insignificant people of the earth, rise to a fulfillment as "the sons and daughters of the living God" made pure and holy through the blood of Jesus Christ, as finally a people with a destiny. The little people of God become His glorious saints, singing with all the redeemed in heaven the song of the Lamb that was slain from the foundation of the world.

Life is a spiritual fellowship. But the spiritual fellowship in life is as weak as men are and with as many foibles and follies as men have. Then along comes death and that fellowship is made perfect and eternal with God in heaven. There is no other way to come to that real communion of saints, where we with all those who are the holy ones, the watchers, stand before His throne, before the throne of the Lamb, forever and ever. This is what Jesus meant when He said, "I am the Resurrection and the Life."

It was an answer, you know, to something Martha had said. But will we first remember that resurrection is always personal in its nature? Resurrection is present in its power in Jesus, because He could not die. The everlasting Son of God, with eternity as part of His soul and being, has made us His members; He says that where He is there is also life and salvation.

Resurrection is also particular in its possibility. Look at it. Listen to it. "He who believes in Me, though he dies, yet shall he live." He who is sure of My power, he who believes that I am eternal, he who believes that I can never perish — him no man shall snatch out of My hands. This resurrection is potent in its promises. "Though he die, yet shall he live." Because he is a part of Me, My eternity is branded on his soul. He is a part of Me, and while I live and where I live "there shall My servant be also." (John 12:26)

Jesus is saying that here is resurrection and life. We do not always need this stated so strongly. In the Gospel lesson of Martha's work and Mary's worship, the Bethany family did not need this comfort couched in calming language. But when we need it, it is there! Just look at the story. Jesus was beyond the Jordan, about 30 or 35 miles away. He could have gotten to Bethany sooner, but instead he waited two days before even beginning the journey. When He came, Lazarus had already been dead for four days and put away in his grave. When He did come, Jesus stayed outside the village at Lazarus' grave. He did not go into the little village to the house of Mary and Martha, where He knew they would be waiting for Him. When Martha heard that He had come, she rushed out to the grave immediately. Mary, who had been so eager to hear the Lord, sat at home meditating, thinking her own thoughts.

Jesus deals with Martha's doubts and fears in a most remarkable way when, with a faint reproach and a quaver in her voice, she said, "Lord, if You had been here, my brother would not have died." Jesus looked at her and said, "Your brother will rise again." Martha says, "Yes, I know all about that." Most likely even the rabbi had said that. "I know that he will rise again in the resurrection at the Last Day." And then Jesus, without any further explanation, says, "I am the Resurrection and the Life." This Resurrection, Martha, is personal. It is not at the Last Day. "I am the Resurrection and the Life; he who believes in Me, though he die, yet shall he live, and whosoever lives and believes in Me shall never die. Do you believe this?"

I wonder what we would answer if He came and asked us so bluntly, "Do you believe this? Do you really believe that because you are members of Mine, you will never die?" Martha, as baffled as we, said, "Yes, Lord, I believe that You are the Christ, the Son of God, He who is coming into the world." She was saying with this that so many things might happen because the Son of God is come into the world, because God has reached down into history, because God has intervened in the things that we accepted as normal before. Maybe she had even heard His sermon right outside Bethany, when He said, "I came that they may have life and have it abundantly" (John 10:10). But she was too confused just now to understand it all. I think we are often confused too.

What about our faith for hard days? I do not mean the singing faith of Christmas, when everybody joins in, or the singing faith of Easter, when everybody again joins in; I do mean the lonely faith of the hour of bereavement, when love is lost and joy has died. Have we a faith for hard days like that? When the hard days come, do we ask God to do "something special, right now"? Will we remember what Jesus did for Martha then? He did nothing more than to declare the word of life, the same thing that He is doing today and has promised to do till the end of time. When He sent forth His messengers, He told them: "He who hears you, hears Me, and he who rejects you rejects Me, and he who rejects Me rejects Him who sent Me" (Luke 10:16). Do we realize that Christ is doing the same today

when He says, "I am the Resurrection and the Life"?
He is saying that we are members of His. If we are
unconscious of the fact that His life moves in us, we will
always be unhappy at the thought of death. If we know
that we are a part of Him, His body — all of us who
have been redeemed by Him and believe in Him — then
everything grows easy.

Do we realize all this? Are we ready to lay hold on
Him with a steady, strong faith? You see, Lent never
really was meant for the weaklings and the fearful. Going
up to Jerusalem requires that we say it again, "You are
the Christ, the Son of the living God." There is no
way except the way of pain and death for the redemption
of mankind. Christ with you. Christ in you. You in
Christ. Do you feel safe now over against death? Can
you say, "Lord, since you are here and we are here and
we are here together," the way Christ said it to His
heavenly Father, "I in Thee and Thou in Me"? Are we
ready to say it now, "Lord, since You are here, everything must be all right"? My brother, my sister, my
father, my mother, will not die. Can you say it? really
say it? Do you mean it because you are conscious that
the blood of the everlasting Son of God flows in us?
The eternal life that is the power of Him is the power of
us. This is why He redeemed us. "Where I am, there
shall My servant be also" (John 12:26). Can the Head
arise and leave the members dead?

Perhaps a Christian missionary, a German caught
behind the bamboo curtain by Chinese communists and
sure that he would die within a few days, said it best.
They wrote to him and asked whether he wasn't afraid

of the things that were going to happen. He wrote it
down beautifully:

> Afraid of death? Afraid? of what?
> Afraid to see my Savior's face?
> To hear His welcome and to trace
> The glory gleams from wounds of grace?
> Afraid? Afraid of that?
>
> If death is to enter the City
> And be hailed as the child of the King,
> O grave, where sounds thy triumph?
> O death, where hides thy sting?

Grace Is Enough

(death of a young man after months of suffering)

2 Corinthians 11:30; 12:9-12   Ronald C. Starenko

The words of our text apply in a unique way to our concern right now. They offer an answer to a question that is puzzling all of us.

Carl was only 39 years old, and to us that seems too young to die. We may try to accept his comparatively early death with the common saying, "Everybody has to go sometime." Carl wanted to live as much as anyone else, but death comes even to the stoutest of hearts. This much we can acknowledge as inevitable. Carl was a religious man and, like most of us, found religion to be an indispensable part of life. But even the good must go, we tell ourselves.

Somehow such answers do not satisfy. Our basic question, almost a complaint, is what 7 months of repeated setbacks and incessant suffering prove when death comes anyhow. After all our concern and all our prayers, why must we finally submit to this? What is the value of experiencing all this weakness?

I have heard people say that suffering is good for the body or the soul, that it teaches self-control and patience, that it even molds character. Such things we may say as a way of getting around the problem of suffering, but how many of us really believe them? Suffering makes some people bitter and resentful; it can drive them to self-pity and even self-destruction. Suffering does not always end in blessing. Furthermore, we know that we are committed to remove suffering wherever and whenever possible. Human weakness in itself may teach a man something good, but it need not. The problem remains.

In fact, the problem is accentuated the moment we begin to speak of the grace of God. There is much less of a problem for those who have no sincere faith in the love of God, for to them everything may be a dead mechanism with nothing to explain. The believer, on the other hand, is often confused by the seeming contradiction between the suffering of man and the love of God.

Human weakness sometimes seems to be overshadowed by God's strength. It would seem, then, that the strength of God would be more apparent in lives less marked by weakness. This was not so in Carl's case. In one sense, a weaker man you never knew. Many of us knew about him, but few were fully aware of what was happening to him during the last 7 months. Week by week his weakness became more evident, until finally he was stripped of everything commonly associated with strength. He was without physical strength, without a livelihood, without entertainment, cut off from the world, without all the things that are part of our fast, furious, fat suburban living. He was stripped to the bone, literally and figuratively. What was left?

The grace of God remained. All Carl's suffering and weakness illustrated that if a man has the love of God as a living reality in Christ, that is enough. This is certainly not to despise the blessings we enjoy in life. Even Paul did not welcome pain. He prayed that his "thorn in the flesh," whatever it was, would pass, but it stuck with him through all his other hardships and persecutions and sufferings. The value of his trials was that in the midst of the worst kind of weakness he discovered the sufficiency of God's grace and came to know that in his own weakness the power of Christ was being made perfect.

What is more, when a man lives long with suffering, he often comes to know himself better. He discovers many of his false values, his false trust. He becomes increasingly aware of his own helplessness, his creatureliness, and his sinfulness. He is brought face to face with his essential weakness. With all his strength drained, he has no defense but Jesus Christ. During these last 7 months Carl grew in his conviction that God's grace was sufficient for him.

Why is the grace of God enough? It is because God accepts us in our weakness. Instinctively we want to make ourselves seem stronger than we are. We do not want our weakness exposed; we would rather display and boast of strength. Indeed, by nature we are set against facing and confessing our weakness. For this reason we resist grace till God exposes our weakness and reveals His strength. Then God's strength can become not our undoing but our remaking. His power is made perfect in weakness. How precious for us is that period of apparent weakness when Christ Himself hung suffering the cross even to death. In the regathered vitality of His resurrection the Christ renounces cruel death and in love announces that He, far from despising and deserting us in our weakness, imparts to us His divine strength. Christ's assurance of love and forgiveness is enough. It was enough for the apostle Paul. It was and is enough for our Carl.

It is enough for us too. It's enough for you, Wilma.

You feel weak now, but the power of Christ is being made perfect in you. As we sing in one of our hymns,

> When every earthly prop gives way,
> He then is all my Hope and Stay.

TLH 370:3

These are not idle words. They express the sure Word of the Gospel. Christ accepts us as we are and turns us into His likeness. Here lies the secret of God's power in our lives. When we were without life or strength of our own, He made us. When we took the life and strength He gave but then used it for ourselves against Him in the weakness of sin, He rescued us. When we could not by our own reason or strength believe in Jesus Christ, He called us by the Gospel. And when we fall victim to the final weakness of death itself, He will be our resurrection and life. We, the living or the dead, have been given the power of Christ, and His grace is enough.

A Passing Guest
(death from incurable illness)

Psalm 39:12   George J. Maassel

Life in this world presents a variety of offenses as stumbling blocks to the child of God. David speaks of some of them in Psalm 39. He mentions the wicked who are before him (v. 1). There is so much evil in the world; in the words of the apostle John, the whole world lies in wickedness. And often it seems that the wicked get away with their wickedness. Equally disturbing for Christians are the afflictions of life, which Paul assures us are light and momentary but which sometimes seem to weigh heavy without lifting. David laments: "Behold, Thou hast made my days a few handbreadths, and my lifetime is as nothing in Thy sight. Surely every man stands as a mere breath! Surely man goes about as a shadow! Surely . . . man heaps up and knows not who will gather" (vv. 5-6). The Christian, brought low by his burden of daily sin, must also plead with David: "Deliver me from all my transgressions. Make me not the scorn of the fool!" (v. 8). Earlier in this penitential psalm David prays: "Lord, let me know my end and what is the measure of my days; let me know how fleeting my life is!" (v. 4). Because of these pleas Luther has described this psalm as "a prayer for the true art of dying, as a sure medicine against offense."

Our departed brother had occasion, by the grace of God, to pray for this true art of dying. The last years of his life give indication that God also heard his prayers. About two years ago he became ill and felt that there was no help left for him. Only reluctantly he entered the hospital for extensive surgery. To his own and his friends' amazement, his recovery was remarkable. But when a year later the same affliction again appeared, our brother withdrew more and more to himself. The last few months he seldom left his house. How much he appreciated it when his pastor visited him with the assurances of God's grace and mercy. But of his serious illness he said little, insisting that he was getting along all right. It was quite apparent that he expected no miraculous cure. He was waiting for the Lord to summon him to Himself in heaven. His thoughts and desires are well expressed in the words of our text: "Hear my prayer, O Lord, and give ear to my cry; hold not Thy peace at my tears! For I am Thy passing guest, a sojourner, like all my fathers."

In this hour of leave-taking let us meditate on these words and learn how fitting and comforting they are for the child of God.

When we read and hear these words, we may get the impression that David is uncertain about the outcome of his outcry to God. The words sound as though David supposes God has not been listening, that He has turned a deaf ear to his cry and closed His eyes without response to the tears of His petitioner. But there is a difference between the abandonment a helpless man feels and the attention God devotes to His children's appeals. David does not deceive himself as to his condition. In the foregoing verses he says: "Remove Thy stroke from me; I am spent by the blows of Thy hand. When Thou dost chasten man with rebukes for sin, Thou dost consume like a moth what is dear to him; surely every man is a mere breath!" (Vv. 10 to 11)

David knows from whom his adversity comes. What he feels are the blows of God's hand. God is rebuking and correcting him, and God has reason to do so. He chastises David because of his iniquity. But when this happens to David, when he is made to feel God's hand heavy upon him, he does not turn away from God. He does not say: "It's no use to call on God for help. He is determined to hurt me even more, and eventually He will be done with me in death." In short, David reacts to God not according to what he feels God does in discipline at the moment but according to God's unfailing promises. Let us not forget that the David who speaks in this psalm is the same who in Psalm 51:14-15 declared: "Deliver me from blood-guiltiness, O God, Thou God of my salvation, and my tongue will sing aloud of Thy deliverance. O Lord, open Thou my lips, and my mouth shall show forth Thy praise." He is the same David who said in Psalm 32:1: "Blessed is he whose transgression is forgiven, whose sin is covered." He is the same David who confidently asserted in Psalm 23:6: "Surely goodness and mercy shall follow me all the days of my life, and I shall dwell in the house of the Lord forever."

So David prayed: "Hear my prayer, O Lord, and give ear to my cry; hold not Thy peace at my tears!" He grew in confidence that God did give ear to his cry and that God would not ignore his tears. That he was in great distress did not cause David to cease praying; rather, it lent his pleadings an urgency that he otherwise might not have felt. God did hear his prayer, much as the Lord heard the prayer of the apostle Paul and responded to his plea with the words: "My grace is sufficient for you, for My power is made perfect in weakness." (2 Cor. 12:9)

How well our brother learned David's art of praying. God had spared him, granting him recovery from his first severe illness. But when his affliction reappeared, our brother's prayers were in the spirit of David's appeal. No longer did he pray that he might again be spared and recover his strength; his prayer was rather that God would teach him the true art of dying as a medicine against offense. In so praying he found strength in his weakness. With David he could add: "For I am Thy passing guest, a sojourner, like all my fathers."

The two terms guest ("stranger" KJV) and sojourner apparently had special meaning for David. These same two words he used is his prayer of thanksgiving when the people brought abundant offerings for the building of the temple. On that occasion David said: "We are strangers before Thee, and sojourners, as all our fathers were; our days on the earth are like a shadow, and there is no abiding" (1 Chron. 29:15). The two words are closely related. The stranger is a resident, not a native. The sojourner is a settler who has come from another land. Of Abraham, Isaac, and Jacob we read in the Scriptures that they sojourned in the promised land, that they dwelt there in tabernacles or tents. Not even their dwellings suggested permanent residence. David's terms imply two facts. The first is stated in a pastoral letter by Paul: "We brought nothing into the world, and we cannot take anything out of the world" (1 Tim. 6:7). The second is expressed by the writer of the Letter to the Hebrews (13:14): "Here we have no lasting city, but we seek the city which is to come." In his prayer David was not asking that his life be pro-

longed. He asked only that God remember his status as
a stranger and sojourner who was willing and ready to
leave all his earthly possessions behind and return to his
true home empty-handed, as did the prodigal son.

Our departed brother subscribed to these words. Although God had blessed him with a measure of this world's
goods, he did not cling to them. He knew with the insight
of a New Testament Christian that his true citizenship is in
heaven. He looked for the Savior, the Lord Jesus Christ,
who could change his mortal body to be like His own glorious body. How aware he was of being a stranger and
sojourner in this world, but he also knew his real destination, his true home. He was mindful of the words of Paul
to the Ephesians (2:19-22): "So then you are no longer
strangers and sojourners, but you are fellow citizens with
the saints and members of the household of God, built
upon the foundation of the apostles and prophets, Christ
Jesus Himself being the cornerstone, in whom the whole
structure is joined together and grows into a holy temple
in the Lord; in whom you also are built into it for a dwell-
ing place of God in the Spirit."

During the last weeks of our brother's life, both his body
and his house took on more and more the appearance of
a tent, a temporary abode that he would exchange for a
mansion in the Father's house. He knew that Jesus is the
Way, the Truth, and the Life. He was confident that Jesus
had gone to prepare a place for him. Thus, through the
Word of God and under the guidance of the Spirit, our
brother learned the true art of dying as a sure medicine
against offense. With the hymn writer Paul Gerhardt he
could say:

A pilgrim and a stranger,
I journey here below;
Far distant is my country,
The home to which I go.
Here I must toil and travail,
Oft weary and opprest;
But there my God shall lead me
To everlasting rest.

There I shall dwell forever,
No more a parting guest,
With all Thy blood-bought children
In everlasting rest,
The pilgrim toils forgotten,
The pilgrim conflicts o'er,
All earthly griefs behind me,
Eternal joys before.

TLH 586:1, 7

The Rock Higher Than I

(for a suicide)

Psalm 61:1-2   Alfred Doerffler

A tragedy, overwhelming and staggering, has come into your life. You are stunned and distracted, but by the grace of God you are not in despair. The greater the sorrow, so much greater the power of God to give you the faith that makes you more than conqueror. This faith enables you to look up and hope.

The tragedy is so much greater because you lived so happily in your 20 years of marriage. Your love and devotion to one another has been sincere, growing and deepening as the years went by. You were drawn closer and closer to one another through the trials, disappointments, problems, and sorrows you had to face through the years. Together you found strength, encouragement, and comfort in the Gospel of Jesus Christ. Your devotion to your husband in the days of his illness revealed that Christian faith developed loyalties that cannot be undermined by the hardships of life.

The tragedy has stunned and shocked you because your husband throughout life proved himself to be deeply religious, and regularly attended the divine services until his health failed him. Even during his illness he gave himself daily to prayers and the reading of God's Word. When we visited him from time to time, he expressed his appreciation for the prayers offered for his well-being. From a child he knew the Holy Scripture and found guidance and encouragement in its promises.

Therefore the only explanation for this tragic act is to be found in an illness that upset his nervous system and brought on depressive moods, confusing his thinking. He lost all sense of responsibility, and his conduct often was strange and abnormal. In all charity and love we want to believe that because of his nervous collapse and physical breakdown he lost all sense of values and was not responsible for his actions. We leave, then, the entire matter in the hands of God and know that He in His grace understands. He is merciful and full of sympathy. Each child of His in distress He makes acceptable through Jesus Christ.

This takes the sting out of this tragic hour. We are troubled and sorrowful but not in despair. We can and do come to the one place, the Rock that is higher than we, our Refuge in this tragic hour. So we pray: O God, "from the end of the earth I call to Thee when my heart is faint. Lead Thou me to the Rock that is higher than I."

In this prayer we make a confession. We admit that we cannot cope with this situation in our own strength. Our own helplessness is apparent. Our friends stand at our side, unable to do anything in their mute silence. There is an aloneness and weakness which makes the days that lie ahead dark and gloomy, without a ray of sunshine breaking through the clouds of sorrow.

However, in this prayer we also confess our faith. We believe that all things, even tragedies of life, are in the hands of God. Even though many things happen to us which are catastrophic, one thing cannot happen to us — we shall not perish. This is the promise Jesus makes to us at the present moment: Whoever believes in God's only Son will not perish but have eternal life.

We believe that God is our Higher Rock in time of trouble. He will uphold us amid the swellings of Jordan. Therefore we can hold fast to God's faithfulness and His promises. He will save us to the uttermost. So we pray: Lead me to the Rock that is higher than my troubles.

In this prayer we make a plea. We ask for help. We pray to God that He will give us a faith that remains unshaken by this tragic act, that He will give us a hope that takes us to, and reaches into, the eternity of glory. With this we find peace of heart and mind.

We pray that God will banish from our minds every thought that may embitter our lives and make us rebellious as we face future problems of life. God must take you by the hand and guide you through the trying days of adjustment.

We plead for comfort. Only God can heal the bruised heart and open our eyes to see that He is still with us, that He is a God who in Christ Jesus does not forsake us in the lonely hours when life seems empty and meaningless.

We ask for assurance. We plead that God will let us experience the blessedness of His grace, that He will give to us each day His renewed strength, which will enable us to carry on. Above all, we need every day the assurance of His forgiving love, revealed to us through the cross of Calvary. So we plead: Lead me to the Rock that is higher than my sorrows.

This Higher Rock sent His Son in the fullness of time into this world of sin and trouble to become "the Rock of Ages," Christ Jesus. This Jesus is our Shepherd, who guides us from day to day in the paths of Christian living.

Therefore we are not alone with our problems. His bene-
dictions are assured us by His continual presence. This
Jesus is our understanding Friend, who sympathizes with
us as we face the vexing situations of life and places under-
neath His everlasting arms to uphold us. No matter what
the burden may be which wants to crush us, He gives us
the needed faith to stand up under the trials confronting us.
This Jesus, above all, is our Savior, who has redeemed us
with His own blood, blots out all our sins, and gives us
that peace which passes understanding. No matter what
we must face in this life, God is reconciled to us through
His Son. He has made full atonement for all our sins.
Truly you can face life with renewed courage as long as
Jesus is your Rock of Ages and the Lover of your soul.

Dazed, mystified, distressed, in tears, now and always
you can seek Him who says to you: Come to Me, and find
rest for your soul. You cannot despair or look hopelessly
ahead as long as you can reach up to the Higher Rock
with the prayer:

> Rock of Ages, cleft for me,
> Let me hide myself in Thee.
> *TLH* 376:1

A Sorrow Too Great for Tears
(suicide of a church elder)

John 5:24   Walter F. Troeger

The most beautiful life, when the course of its hours is run, comes to an end. The most dedicated, gentle, and useful life, when its divinely appointed mission is fulfilled and its divinely measured span — long or short — is completed, comes to its close. Life is an irreplaceable gift of God. Whatever our trials and tribulations may be, it is not a matter of our choosing to terminate our earthly existence before time, so long as we are in responsible control of our faculties.

Mary stood beneath the Cross with a sorrow too great for tears. Great nails had pierced her Savior's hands and feet, and the sword spoken of by the aged Simeon had pierced her soul. Yet she kept the faith. She stood by unflinching, and in due time Good Friday was followed by Easter.

In this uncertain life, death may suddenly crash into our home and the circle of our friends without notice, and we stand mute before the unsearchable counsels of God. Our heavenly Father sometimes washes the eyes of His saints with tears that they may see more clearly the boundaries and power of His redeeming love.

Physicians tell us of the metabolism of the body. If that perfect balance is upset, the whole body may be affected and its strength and normal functions impaired. How true this may be also of that intricate organism, the human mind. In a dream, we may vividly see persons long dead. We may converse with them and have dealings with them in a seemingly logical way, yet reason may be asleep and not at the helm.

When the mind is troubled, affected by shock or great pain or an approaching nervous collapse, normal thought processes and sound Christian judgment may be momentarily suspended, if not permanently and completely dethroned.

We mourn today the loss of a young husband and father, a devoted son and brother. Our hearts go out in deepest sympathy to the bereaved. We also mourn in him the passing of a precious friend, a consecrated Christian leader in civic, professional, military, and church circles. During his 15 years in this community, including 4 years in his country's service as an Air Force officer, he endeared himself to many hearts, which now painfully feel a great loss.

Sometimes events take such a turn in life that we stand deeply humbled; we do not have the answer. We are compelled to withhold judgment and must leave that to God alone. In his First Letter to the Corinthians (4:5), Paul writes: "Therefore do not pronounce judgment before the time, before the Lord comes, who will bring to light the things now hidden in darkness and will disclose the purposes of the heart. Then every man will receive his commendation from God."

The text before us takes for granted that there is to be a day of condemnation, of supreme and final judgment. Our own conscience bears witness forcibly to this fact, for we ourselves best know our many sins and shortcomings. Our sense of justice also tells us that there must be a day of retribution for the wicked who troubled and tormented their fellowmen or otherwise fattened on the woes and miseries of mankind. And there must come a day of relief for the oppressed who trusted in God, suffering wrongfully, and were faithful to their last responsible moment.

Holy Scripture certifies from Genesis to Revelation that God will judge the world. "He has fixed a day on which He will judge the world in righteousness by a Man whom He has appointed, and of this He has given assurance to all men by raising Him from the dead." (Acts 17:31)

It is clear that Christians, too, must appear before the judgment seat of Christ. "The hour is coming when all who are in the tombs will hear His voice and come forth" (John 5:28-29). "Each of us shall give account of himself to God. Then let us no more pass judgment on one another" (Rom. 14:12-13). "We must all appear before the judgment seat of Christ so that each one may receive good or evil, according to what he has done in the body." (2 Cor. 5:10)

Weighed on the scale of justice, we are compelled to cry out with the psalmist: "If Thou, O Lord, shouldst mark iniquities, Lord, who could stand?" (Ps. 130:3). By every law of right and justice, we have to acknowledge that we are by nature lost and sold under sin and subject to condemnation.

The physician who attended the deceased and who knew him well, stated his opinion briefly. He summed it up in two words: "Something snapped." We believe that in the final judgment God will hold us accountable on the basis of what we were and what we believed in our last lucid and responsible moments, not on what we may have said or done after that.

The time will come when the things that seem so important to us in life will be important no longer. What will be important in the end is that we cling in childlike faith to the Word before us, which we have from the lips of God's own Son: "Truly, truly, I say to you, he who hears My Word and believes Him who sent Me has eternal life; he does not come into judgment but has passed from death to life." (John 5:24)

Above the din and roar of condemnation, this beautiful message comes to our troubled spirits with the breath of springtime. It comes with a glorious promise. It comes with the sound of opening prison doors. It comes with blessed assurance, verified by the Son of God. Hearing and believing this Gospel promise is more wondrous and beautiful than stepping out into a clear night and seeing the stars of heaven in all their celestial glory.

Christ Jesus, the Lamb of God, came into the world to save sinners. He redeemed us to God by His blood. If we but hear His Word and believe in Him as our only Savior, we shall be accounted righteous in His sight and will not come into condemnation, not be judged and condemned on that great Day. Our sins will not again be uncovered, for God has canceled, forgiven, and forgotten them for Jesus' sake.

During his lifetime the deceased knew and loved the Lamb of God. He heard the Word and followed the voice of the Good Shepherd. He was brought to Jesus in his infancy on the arms of prayer and through Holy Baptism. He was reared in a Christian home, a Lutheran parsonage, and trained in a parish school. His whole life long he remained an active member of his Savior's church, taking an interest in its problems and plans, supporting it according to his means, attending divine services faithfully, serving for a number of seasons as a Bible class leader and for 3 years as an elder.

Our dear departed brother gave many evidences of his belief in God and his devotion to duty at home and in the service. He really loved and used his service Bible and his Lutheran Prayer Manual. A few Sundays ago he partook of Holy Communion with his wife and fellow Christians. Before the world he was not ashamed of the Gospel of Christ but freely spoke of his church and his Savior.

It is evident from office records that the deceased, to his very last day, planned not to die but to live and work. An agreement was signed and a check issued for the rental of enlarged facilities. Additional equipment and carpeting was ordered, and arrangements were completed for adding a co-worker to his firm. Yes, hours before his death, he agreed to meet a business friend at a later time, and there were other appointments and commitments, business and religious.

If in his last moments of full consciousness and accountability our late brother in Christ still held to the Word of God in his heart and believed on Him who sent us the Savior, all the precious Gospel promises apply to him. "He has passed from death to life." Jesus also said: "I am the Resurrection and the Life; he who believes in Me, though he die, yet shall he live." (John 11:25)

The sudden, tragic passing of our beloved brother teaches us all a most important lesson. Let us hear the Word of God while we may. Let us repent and believe and worship God while we are able to go to His house and while we are of sound mind. "He who has ears to hear, let him hear!" (Matt. 11:15)

We are living in troublous times of national and international upheaval, of wars and rumors of wars, of wickedness and fraud in high places, of false prophets and deceivers, of atheism and atheistic communism threatening to overrun the world. If ever there was a time for Christians to hear the Word of God, to reaffirm their faith in Jesus Christ, to stand firmly and to stand together, it is now.

May the Holy Spirit in mercy abundantly comfort the bereaved and in His own way and time heal the deep wound which this tragedy has caused in church and family circles. We humbly confess that the Lord knows best. We place our future in His hands, whether our remaining days be many or few. To this end we pray:

> My faith looks up to Thee,
> Thou Lamb of Calvary,
> Savior divine.
> Now hear me while I pray;
> Take all my guilt away;
> Oh, let me from this day
> Be wholly Thine!

TLH 394:1

The Wages and the Gift

(one who killed his wife and committed suicide)

Romans 6:23   Herbert F. Lindemann

The function of the church on an occasion of this kind
is not to condone or excuse sin. As the body of Christ
in the world, that is never its intention. The church is
the mouthpiece of God and therefore must, as its bounden
duty, reflect and rehearse His justice in all its terrible
severity. It dare not say concerning the present tragic
circumstance that the justice of God has nothing to do
with it. To say such a thing would not only be a betrayal
of a solemn responsibility; it would run counter to the
feeling we all have.

The tragedy of last Saturday morning came as a great
shock to this city, particularly to you who for various
reasons were somewhat close to these young people or
to their families. If you analyze that feeling carefully, you
will perceive that it is a jolting realization of what terrible
results sin produces in the world. Tragedies like these
result from sin, as they have in thousands of similar
situations since the beginning of time. It is all of a piece:
the wholesale sin of which we have read in other parts
of the world and the more private evil that at a time like
this directly affects our lives. Let it be understood that
I am not speaking merely of whatever sin was committed
early Saturday morning. Included are the evil circumstances which preceded that occurrence, the attitudes,

thought-patterns, and habits which these young people unconsciously adopted from this pagan world, as well as the sin with which they were born. Included are also ungodly impulses, desires, thoughts, words, and deeds which you and I like to call by softer names than those applied to them by the Lord of justice, but which are condemned by Him in the severest and most uncompromising terms. Sin abounds in our world, and sin abounds in us, and the wages of sin is death. There is no good in blinking at these unpalatable but all too evident facts.

The function of the church, however, is not to pass judgment on souls that have passed into eternity. That is the prerogative of God alone; He has not delegated it to human beings. The church has merely been assigned the duty of preaching the truth. The truth we have been commissioned to proclaim is concerned mainly with the two great facts spoken of in our text: the facts of sin and grace. The preaching of sin takes on added force when such a startling illustration is before us as it is today. Death is always a proof of the power of sin, particularly when it has been brought about by the hand of man. You and I have no way of knowing, of course, the degree or the variety of mental disturbance that drove this young man to do what he did; nor can we form any accurate estimate of how much the young woman's attitude contributed to his state of mind. We all agree that something has been done which should not have been done, that for some time past there have existed between these two people circumstances which should not have existed, that words were uttered and courses of action initiated which were not according to the spirit of Christ. These are the facts of the matter, and it is both useless and cowardly to ignore them. They are summed up in the ugly word "sin," the wages of which, as we all see only too plainly, is death.

All of this must, however, be said penitently. Someone remarked to me, upon hearing of this tragedy, "I thank God that nothing like that could ever happen to my husband and me." Couldn't it? There, but for the grace of God, lie you and I! We are made of no different stuff than these two. Were they sinners? So are we. Did they break God's law? So do we. Are they deserving of His terrible wrath and punishment? So are we. Have they come before the bar of His exact judgments? So must we. Human beings differ from one another by the degree of their sin, but not in kind. All of it is traceable to the same source, and all of it, but for divine grace, has the same end. The most highly respected of us are potentially the worst criminals. We are born with the tendency. In some it has consequences which are more apparent, that's all. And with none of it, big or small, hidden or evident, publicized in the newspapers or concealed in the heart — with none of it will the holy God have anything to do. That's one thing.

But, thank heaven, there is another: though the wages of sin may be death, "the free gift of God is eternal life in Christ Jesus our Lord" (Rom. 6:23). Or as Paul also states it, "Where sin increased, grace abounded all the more" (5:20). It had to be so, God being the kind of God He is. Justice is one side of His nature; love is another. Because both were a part of His being, Christ came into the world to take the full weight of justice and judgment on Himself and thereby to relieve us of it, so demonstrating the infinite compassion of God. This, above all else, is the truth which the church lives to proclaim.

For many of you, no doubt, the Gospel of redemption from sin is the heart of your religion, the ground of your faith, the basis of your hope. I refer you to it again in the face of what has occurred. Everyone of us is sorely puzzled as to why God permitted this tragedy. At first glance, there seems to be no benefit that accrues to anyone connected with it. On reflection, however, certain rocklike truths begin to emerge from the pit, to the brink of which two families have suddenly been brought. One of these truths is that we have been given an awful power to do with our lives as we will, to live for God or for Satan or to put an end to life entirely. But a still more towering fact is the evangelical truth that into the course of sin and hell-bent human living the good God has interposed Himself by sending into the world His only-begotten Son and by that Son's offering of Himself on the altar of the cross. By that act of redemption the mind and heart of God are revealed to us. By this we may know what He is like, how He feels toward us, what He wishes for our life in this world and in the next. Here is the unchanging fact of divine love, which any man may perceive and receive by a faithful following of the direction of the forerunner's finger. "Behold, the Lamb of God, who takes away the sin of the world!" (John 1:29)

To you who may be inclined to doubt the love of God because of what has happened, the fact of Christ crucified looms up as the enduring testimony of it. What occurred on Calvary is a historical fact. The infinite compassion of it has not changed since Good Friday, for He who hung on the cross is "the same yesterday and today and forever" (Heb. 13:8). Unchanged too is His ability to turn such horror as crucifixion into a resurrection that spells salvation. He will do that for you, if you will let Him. "All things work together for good to them that love God" (Rom. 8:28), even such a thing as the untimely and tragic death of this husband and wife, this father and mother, this son and daughter. May it be so for you, the members of their immediate families. God's will, so mysterious in some ways, is perfectly clear in this, that through suffering He means to bring us closer to Himself, into the fellowship of the suffering of His Son. You and I dare not frustrate His purpose or refuse to let His will be done in us. What has happened has not happened without some gracious intention for us. If we do not learn the lesson which He proposes to teach, then all this has been in vain, a very meaningless occurrence indeed.

One more thing: If for any here present the grace of God is a phrase and not a living reality, this tragedy should serve as a potent jolt to move them to put themselves at the receiving end of it. In the catechism used in our church, it is stated that the purpose of our Savior's atonement was that we might be delivered from "the guilt, the punishment, and the dominion of sin." For this gracious purpose to be realized, it is necessary that the grace of God be made use of by an act of faith. Its established channels of Word and Sacrament have their intended outlets in the souls of each of us. What our Savior did on Calvary and what His Spirit is still willing to do in our souls must not be allowed to go to waste. Grace abounds that "as sin reigned in death, grace also might reign through righteousness to eternal life through Jesus Christ our Lord. . . . But now that you have been set free from sin and have become slaves of God, the return you get is sanctification and its end, eternal life. For the wages of sin is death, but the free gift of God is eternal life in Christ Jesus our Lord" (Rom. 5:21; 6:22-23). If this gift is not yours, accept it. If you do not enjoy this freedom or bring this service, begin today. If this fruit does not grow on the tree of your life, see to it. Otherwise your being here today will have done you no good.

So we lay the bodies of these two young people to rest. Concerning the present and eternal state of their souls the church does not presume to make pronouncements. But this it does say most emphatically, that the state of the souls of us who remain should give us all most serious concern. If those two deaths do not bring us closer to God, nothing is likely to do it. "We must all appear before the judgment seat of Christ so that each one may receive good or evil, according to what he has done in the body. Therefore, knowing the fear of the Lord, we persuade men. . . . We are ambassadors for Christ, God making His appeal through us. We beseech you on behalf of Christ, be reconciled to God. For our sake He made Him to be sin who knew no sin, so that in Him we might become the righteousness of God." And "we make it our aim to please Him." (2 Cor. 5: 10-11, 20-21, 9)

The Benediction of Sorrow

(memorial for college students killed in automobile accident)

Revelation 5:12; 7:17   O. P. Kretzmann

Whenever death comes to a Christian as it came to our friends a few weeks ago, it never brings only a single gift. It always carries more than one thing. In the Christian view it carries joy, peace, glory, and rest to the soul which is now free of the chains of mortality and ready to see God as we have not yet seen Him. We must never forget that in the Christian view death brings no sorrow to those sons and daughters of Christ who die. Death brings sorrow only to those who live. To those of us who remain here for a little while it brings a cup of tears, a seemingly bitter gift, the ultimate myrrh of life and living.

And so in these few brief moments this morning I do not want to talk about our friends and fellow students. They died as Christians. The tremendous effective operation of God's Holy Spirit brought them in their dying moments the memory of their childhood faith, of Christian homes where Christ was at home, of Christian parents and teachers who had kept them close to the cross. And so they are very content and very happy now. They came to the end of the road sooner than they or we had expected, but as they know now, that does not really matter. The end, whenever in life and time it comes, is always the same for the Christian — God and heaven and joy and peace. We know that because at the end what matters is not that we hold God but that He holds us.

I believe, therefore, that our friends would be the first to say that we should now think of ourselves. For us death also has a gift, but it is not easy to appreciate. Someone has said that death always makes philosophers of men. That is true. More than any other event in human existence it compels us to ask why. I am sure that everyone on our campus has asked this question again and again during the past two weeks: "Why? Why did it happen? Why did they, so young and so happy, have to die?" We all know, of course, that the question is not new. It has been asked by men since our first parents stood outside the gates of paradise lost. It is the great tolling question of the universe and of time — from palace and hut, from young and old, from rich and poor, from great and lowly it rises to the throne of judgment and of mercy. It is the great wailing cry of children lost in the night: "Why does God permit certain things to happen? Why all the pain and heartaches that follows the evening sun across the world?" More than any other fact in life death brings us face to face with this question. This is it! This is the ultimate barrier between the mind of man and the mind of God. There must be a way across or through it if we are to live sanely and happily; in fact, if we are to live at all. Without some answer, life would be desolation. It would become a world of broken hearts and empty arms, cruel, senseless, brutal, and blind, utterly without meaning and without hope.

For one and only one type of person there is an answer. It is an answer not of logic or reason or philosophy. It is the answer that is the great benediction of sorrow even of the final sorrow of death. It is the blessed assurance, beyond tears and beyond hope, brought by the power of the Spirit of God, that God is in this! It is the knowledge that He uses even death to bring the golden gift of a stronger faith and surer hope. It is the sureness that the cleansing fire of sorrow leaves not ashes but warmth — the strange warmth that comes from our God-given knowledge of the fact that God loves us — loves us enough to blind our eyes with tears that we may see Him more clearly — loves us enough to break our hearts so that they will be mended in Him — loves us enough to remind us again and again that we have here no continuing city — that life is a pilgrimage whose length is uncertain but whose end is sure.

This, I would like to suggest to you, is the meaning of the seeming tragedy that has come over us. This is the benediction of sorrow! If it does not mean this, what in the name of God can it mean? There is only one other possible answer — the answer which so many in our generation have given — that all of this really means nothing, that it is no more and no less than the crushing of an insect under our feet, the falling of a leaf, or the withering of a flower. I prefer, and I think you should too this morning, the other answer that God is in this and that beyond the white stillness of death is the white mercy of God over a cross, holding our friends now and all of us in His everlasting arms, giving them the benediction of glory and the rest of us the benediction of sorrow and of hope.

In the light of that twofold benediction we know exactly what happened the evening of April 13 on a Wisconsin road. An angel stood before the throne of God, white and still, and the voice of God came to him: "I have some children down there now who are ready to come home." And so there was another presence on the dark highway that night, standing invisible among on-lookers, police and the curious crowd that always gathers at such accidents. At God's own moment the angel took their souls into his hands and began the long journey upward — beyond the stars, beyond all worlds, beyond all time, to the eternal presence of God. The journey began in darkness, the darkness of earth and of sin, of Friday night, April 13. But as the angel flew there was a great and greater light, brighter, whiter, stronger, until the whole universe was full of the searching majesty and mercy of God Himself. The angel came to the throne of God with the souls of our friends and left them there. God looked at them, not for the first time. He had seen them and loved them from all eternity. They, however, looked at God for the first time, and what they saw we cannot imagine. But what they heard we know. They heard the great choirs of heaven chanting: "Worthy is the Lamb who was slain, to receive power and wealth and wisdom and might and honor and glory and blessing!" (Rev. 5:12). And God bent down from His throne and wiped away all tears from their eyes. And they knew no more sorrow but only benediction. And I am content to leave them there — David, Sandra, Wayne, and Andrew — to say good-bye for a few years in the great words of our liturgy: "Eternal rest grant unto them, O Lord, and let perpetual light shine upon them."

His Balm for Your Bereavement
(memorial for a young theologian)

Rev. 7:15; 1 Cor. 15:20   Herbert E. Hohenstein
John 14:16

God has three things to say to you tonight, three things that constitute His balm for your bereavement. Number one, your loved one and brother received a divine call he simply couldn't turn down. Number two, your reunion is close. Number three, you are not alone.

Henry Reimann was a called man. There is no doubt about that. It wasn't when he graduated from the seminary that he received his first divine call. That happened long ago when his pastor poured the gracious water of life over his head, and thus did God enable baby Henry to celebrate his first glad Epiphany. For in that baptismal act God brought and called our brother out of the dark and terrifying bondage of Satan, hell, death, and sin and into the magnificent and marvelous Epiphany light of His love and grace. How fitting, then, that our glorified brother should reach the goal of this Epiphany act of his baptism on the bright Festival of the Epiphany!

Henry Reimann was a called man, called by God to be a saint. Here is a description of this man, composed by a member of the faculty of Concordia Teachers College, River Forest, Ill.:

> Henry Reimann had come to represent, for those who had grown up with him in the past two and a half

decades in the church, all that is the finest in the traditions of The Lutheran Church — Missouri Synod. As scholar and teacher, as pastor and theologian, Henry Reimann, with a deep sense of history, participated in the past, agonized in the present, and rejoiced in the future. His life was molded as much by worship as by academic discipline. His books became hymnals, his desk an altar. Henry Reimann lived long enough and worked hard enough to mark the lives of those who have known him with the indelible lines of the figure of the Servant he served, the Savior who summons to faith, to faithfulness, to death in life, and life in death. The students and faculty and Board of Control of Concordia Teachers College, River Forest, Ill., experienced the blessing of Henry Reimann's teaching and presence in two summer sessions. We were deeply shocked to learn of his sudden death. To his colleagues and most especially to his family we express our profoundest conviction that Henry preferred, as the true theologian he was, the crown of life to the doctor's hood.

Henry Reimann was called to be a saint, and that meant his entire life was to be a constant Epiphany, a flesh-and-blood mirror and manifestation of his Savior God, and that was surely the case. A few examples, if you please. What Christian courage this man displayed when in the hospital, shortly before his surgery, he handed me, just in case, the directions for his funeral. It wasn't done morbidly, let me assure you. It was done by a brave and valiant saint who had the boldness born of the resurrection hope to stare grim and ugly death right in the eye as the champion, as the victor. Then I think of the words of courage he spoke to me in the hospital. He said: "My wife and I have come to look

upon this sickness as God's great Christmas gift to us."
Think of that. Only a saint could say something like that
about so serious an illness. Henry Reimann was called
to be a saint, and that he surely was.

But he was also called to be a husband and father,
and how diligently, how lovingly, how joyfully he fulfilled
that calling. He was called to be a professor at this seminary, and those of you who worked with him or studied
under him can give glowing and eloquent testimony to
his competence, sincerity, and faithfulness in that voca-
tion. He was also called to be a pastor in Luther Memorial
parish. And who of us, my fellow members at Luther
Memorial, who of us is not closer to his God because of
the preaching and example and ministry of this man?

But it was on the Festival of the Epiphany that our
dear Henry received his last and greatest divine call,
the call to join the happy and glorified saints mentioned
in the Revelation text, who stand and serve God day
and night within His heavenly temple. And, you see,
this was a call that our brother simply couldn't turn down.
It was so grand, so challenging, so glorious — this time
not a call through the human agents of the church but
a direct call from the lips of our Lord Himself. "Oh,
how senseless, how tragic," we are tempted to cry out
in the agony of our bereavement, "that death should take
from the church a theologian and pastor and professor so
young, so vigorous, and so needed!" But let me tell you,
death did not take Henry Reimann from the church.
Death, at the command of the church's Lord, simply
translated our brother into Christ's church triumphant.
And this was a divine call our brother simply couldn't

turn down. May that fact help to comfort our bowed spirits and bleeding hearts.

Here is God's second word of balm for your bereavement. Your reunion is close. The apostle Paul informs us that Jesus Christ burst in glory from His vainly shut and sealed tomb, that He triumphed and championed over a startled and defeated death as the firstfruits of those who sleep. I guess it really isn't planting time, is it? It is only the 9th of January, and yet that is precisely what we have done this day. This afternoon we tenderly and lovingly covered with earth the dormant seed of our brother's body. But please note I said dormant, not dead. For in our brother's baptism Father God combined with Mother Church to bring our brother forth as His own child, and that means the very eternal life of God was pulsing and surging through him. And that life not even the cruel clutch of death can stop or halt. Indeed, it can't. Oh, it's true, the stethoscope found no beat or pulse of life within him. But the same is true of a little dormant seed. By all tests and observations that little seed is absolutely lifeless. But you just put that little seed into the soil and then wait — wait until the soft, gentle rains and the warm spring sun combine to produce the miracle of germination, and then that dormant seed soon pushes up through the soil, bursting out all over with new life. So it will be with our brother, with the dormant seed of his body that we this day have planted. It too, will one day spring up, pulsing and throbbing with new and never-ending life, ready to be harvested together with us all into the granary of heaven.

Let me tell you this. Henry Reimann entered a penitentiary with cracked walls. I am talking about the penitentiary of the tomb. It happened when that Easter earthquake jarred that giant stone loose from the door of Christ's vacated grave. When that happened, that earthquake also put some mighty big, some mighty obvious, some mighty glorious cracks into the penitentiary of death and the grave. Now we know for sure that this jail is doomed to eventual destruction and that our loved ones who now lie chained behind its ugly walls will escape, will be free forever. Henry Reimann entered a jail with cracked walls. Christ, the Firstfruit, has come back from the prison of death. We think here of our Lord's familiar words that the fields are white unto harvest. Indeed they are. The fields that we call cemeteries, with their white tombstones — these fields are white unto the harvest, the harvest of the resurrection. Indeed they are. For even now you can discern with the eyes of faith on these cemetery fields one ripened ear of grain, one Man raised and returned from the silent and gloomy halls of death, Jesus Christ. And that, of course, means that harvest day, resurrection day, is just around the corner. And that, in turn, means that reunion day is mighty close — the deliriously joyful day when you, my dear Margaret and family, will once again embrace in your hungry arms your revived and glorified dear one in God's bright and beautiful new heavens and earth.

> Then eyes with joy shall sparkle
> That brimmed with tears of late;
> Orphans no longer fatherless,
> Nor widows desolate.

TLH 476:3

That day is mighty near. You see it in the raised Christ,

the Christ whom God raised upon the cross, lowered into that rocky garden vault, and then gloriously lifted out again at Easter, that you and I might be raised from the death of our sins to God's own right hand of forgiveness, favor, and eternal fellowship.

This now is God's final word of balm for your bereavement. Jesus says to you, "I will pray the Father, and He will give you another Counselor to be with you forever." Please note, *another* Counselor. That implies that there are two or more, and indeed there are. Jesus, the Counselor of whom the evangelist John speaks when he says that if any man sin, we have a Counselor, a Lawyer, before the Father, Jesus Christ the Righteous. And here is the Lawyer who has never lost a case, the Lawyer who constantly pleads our cause before the Most High, the Lawyer whose constantly folded hands form five crosses as five vivid reminders of the cross He suffered for our salvation. "Now I will pray the Father," says Jesus, "and He will give you *another* Counselor." Oh, it is painfully true that God in His infinite wisdom has taken from you one counselor, your beloved husband, who so often counseled and guided you, sustained you, and sheltered and loved and protected you. But if God has taken one counselor from you, He still lovingly provides you with another, the Holy Spirit. And He, says Jesus, is "to be with you forever." No cruel death can ever rob you of this heavenly Counselor, this heavenly Bystander, this Comforter from on high, who will console and guide and sustain you during these difficult days of your bereavement.

We may think of this Counselor as the first course of God's heavenly meal of gladness and glory, served to us already here and now in time. I guess God isn't like us

parents who so often must send our children away from
the table because they are doing too much predinner
nibbling. God isn't like that. Why, He is so eager to give
us the joys of heaven that He can't wait till we get to the
heavenly banquet table. Already here and now He puts
into our hearts His Holy Spirit, the Comforter. There is
no doubt about it. All of us here, if we persevere in the
faith, are bound to join beloved Henry, feasting in the
eternal banquet hall of heaven. There's no doubt about
it, for we already here and now have the Holy Spirit,
the guarantee of our eternal inheritance.

This, then, is God's balm for your bereavement. Take it!

Shepherd and Sheep — The Saving Bond of Life That Never Dies

(for a young instructor of theology)

Isaiah 40:11; John 10:11, 27-30   Gilbert A. Thiele

I have seen him living. I have seen him working. I have seen him growing as a man, as a Christian, as a teacher. And now I have seen him dying, and I have seen him die.

Walter was born the year I entered the seminary. Both of us, for certain periods during our ministry, served in parishes. His path and mine first crossed at a conference in Michigan in 1957. Thus began the process of the intertwining of our careers and lives in our church and since 1959 at this school. I think, then, that I speak for everyone here: I need hope and comfort, as do my colleagues and you the family, as much as anyone. So I would have you join me in drawing strength, hope, and comfort from these words, taken as they are from both covenants of the Sacred Scriptures, from the Old Testament writer whom we call the evangelist of the Old Covenant and from the New Testament evangelist John.

First it must be said that when we speak of our Blessed Lord, the Savior, as Shepherd, we are dealing with a remarkable paradox and a shift in roles. This morning in this same chapel a sermon was preached on a passage from the first chapter of John's Gospel, where John the Baptist points to our Lord and says, "Behold, the Lamb of God." Yet our Lord gave Himself the title Shepherd and unquestionably named His followers sheep and lambs. There must be some deep reason for this, that He can take upon Himself the role of one who unites himself to his flock as a shepherd really only after He has completely fulfilled His *first* assignment as the Lamb, obedient, tractable, ready to be offered. Only then could He become the Shepherd and establish with His sheep a bond of life that neither breaks nor dies. We belong to Him in His role of Shepherd, which succeeds His labor as the Lamb by right of the redemption that He has achieved.

Everyone likes to have a claim on somebody else, and when we have established a firm claim, especially on someone whom we love, we do not want to see it ever end. When a claim has been established on us by someone good and strong, we would like it to last forever. The bond between the Shepherd and His sheep, established as it is by the redemption that He has achieved, is such a bond that *never* ends. All kinds of similes, metaphors, and figures of speech are used in the Bible to express that God sends His Son to be the Redeemer of the world. Deeply embedded in all of them, in one way or another, is the idea of purchase, gift, offering, sacrifice, or rescue. The very words "redeem," "reclaim," and whatever other synonyms you may know, all have such import. When you can speak of yourselves as the family, as colleagues, or as students and friends or when we, as members of the flock of God, can speak of *Him,* it is only and always because of what first the Savior Himself has done.

This is outlined in John 10:11: "I am the Good Shepherd. The Good Shepherd lays down His life for the sheep." These words apply to all of us surely, but let us now think primarily of Walter. He *was* His and *is* His because of an incalculable price, an unspeakable labor, and an everlasting effort on the part of the Shepherd to add *him* to the number of His own dear sheep. This claim and the right of possession of the Shepherd over us all, His sheep, and above all now over Walter, is not merely something that happened and now just blandly continues. No, it is more.

The verse from Isaiah makes this clear. When sheep belong to the Shepherd and the Shepherd has established His claim on them by right of His redemption, then He continuously works in their behalf. Four wonderful words are used: feed, gather, carry, lead. Certainly these words each have their special application in each individual's life, beginning with the establishment of the lasting claim of the Shepherd on His sheep in the washing by water with the Word. Of this we are convinced. But it does not stop there. I think, perhaps most of all now, of Walter's three boys and their mother and with them especially of these words: "He will gather the lambs in His arms; He will carry them in His bosom and gently lead those that are with young." Where would you, dear sister and daughter in Christ, with your boys be able to find any sense, any meaning, any direction for tomorrow except in just such an assurance that He will work *for* you and *with* you? You can be certain that the boys will not be desolate orphans. While they have lost their father, they will nevertheless be in the very closest association with the Shepherd who has established with them, as He did with their father and has with you, a bond so deep and thorough that we can call it literally everlasting. For the bond between the Lord, the Shepherd, and Walter, His sheep whom we mourn, is not severed. Why, then, should the bond be severed between

the Shepherd and you? between Him and the boys? for
that matter, between the Shepherd and us all?

I suppose it does not often happen on an occasion of
this kind that so many come to participate and share in
your immediate need and grief. Thereby all of us — Walter's parents, your parents, the boys, our students, our
clergy, and our faculty — can find strength. Where will
we find nourishment when we feel as starved as we do
now? Where will we find a haven but in Him who gathers
us in His arms? Where will we find security unless, like
sheep and lambs, we are gathered into that bulky fold in
the garment of the Shepherd of the East as He picks us up?
And where will we find a goal beyond the shock that we
have endured in the last 5 days if He does not lead us as
though we were still young or still expecting children? This
evidence of the ever-present Christ's continuous effort for
us who remain indicates that the bond never breaks or
dies.

In John's Gospel we find assurance that death itself is
not strong enough to break the bond. Our Lord says: "My
sheep hear My voice, and I know them, and they follow
Me; and I give them eternal life, and they shall never perish, and no one shall snatch them out of My hand." We
all feel, somehow or other, that we have become the victims of a monstrous deprivation, for we have lost someone whom we loved and who we know loved us. It is good
to remember that in the memory of those who remain, the
bond remains unbroken. Although it is not a distinctively
Christian concept of immortality, being remembered by
those whom we have left behind does serve a purpose and
has its place. But this also is surpassed by the fact that
death, which takes away from us the normal, everyday,

God-given joys of existence, cannot sever the bond between those who die and Him who saved them. Our whole faith depends ultimately on this truth that the severance, the deprivation, the incision into life that death really is, is for him who dies and for his Savior a reunion, not a separation.

This is of unspeakably great comfort for all of us. Always, especially in cases of sudden death, the very word that Jesus uses is applicable; somebody is snatching these people right out of our lives. We would like to hang onto them, but our hands are empty. Not so the divine hands of the Savior; they are not empty. No death, no evil, no Satan, no hell, can snatch Walter or any of us out of the almighty yet tender hands of the Shepherd. We must remember, too, that Walter has in a very real sense been commended, as so many passages in the Scripture attest, into the hands of God. "Father, into Thy hands," our Lord said (Luke 23:46). Stephen said something similar (Acts 7:59). And generations of Christians all testify that they lived and died in the same confidence in a Christ who will never relinquish them from His hands.

But there is something even greater, if that is possible, than knowing that the bond between the Shepherd and His sheep, between Jesus and Walter, and between Jesus Christ and all of us is a saving bond of life that never breaks or dies. Our Lord says: "My Father, who has given them to Me, is greater than all, and no one is able to snatch them out of the Father's hand. I and the Father are one." We can use, then, from the hymnody of the church such words as "Asleep in Jesus" or any other words of hope with every measure of confidence that this Shepherd is a living, regnant, welcoming Savior. While He is in our midst, He is also at the right hand of God, receiving unto Himself those who were His on earth. It is true that the One who lived, died, rose, and ascended is the One who lived for *us,* died for *us,* and ascended that *we* might follow Him into His mansions.

This is probably as close as we can get in a situation of this kind to any reasonable satisfaction for our minds for the future. Please let us not try to discover the ultimate reason behind an event of this kind. It will elude us. We will despair in the search for the ultimate rationale. But we shall know, and this is God's way with His children.

We here in the seminary have gone through this kind of experience all too often by human standards; in the last 10 years five young men in their late twenties or early thirties have been snatched out of our midst. Perhaps one way of looking at it is this: relatively few are the men whom God allows to finish their work so soon. If it is true that what God wanted Walter to do is finished — we need not now rehearse his activities and achievements — then we can take comfort that he has been taken by the Savior's hands and turned over to the Father's. When you are with Christ, you are with God. It is the same.

For us it might be very difficult for a while. But knowing that the same Savior into whose hands Walter has now been commended is also *our* abiding Shepherd and never-failing Companion and living Lord, we can say: I have seen him living, I have seen him working, I have seen him studying, I have seen him teaching, and I have seen him growing as a man, as a teacher, and as a Christian. This each of us can say, but then we should add: Now let us, in God's name, go on with the business of living and working till this same Shepherd calls us unto Himself.

O God, the Father in heaven, have mercy upon us;
O God, the Son Jesus Christ, Redeemer of the world, have mercy upon us;
O God, the Holy Ghost, the Comforter, have mercy upon us, and grant us Thy peace.

Thy Will Be Done
(death of a pastor after long illness)

Matthew 6:10   F. Dean Lueking

Pastor Geiseman requested this text for this sermon. He has given us the cue for the entire spirit and content of this memorial service. His firm wish was that it center on God and the goodness of His gracious will. Pastor was thinking of us when he chose the text. He knew our needs. He realized that a series of fitting tributes to himself would be of no help or comfort to us in this hour. He did not want the stress to fall on himself and his life; he wanted the emphasis to rest on God and what His will means for us who are still on this side of eternity. Isn't that a faithful pastor's wish, that his people be fed and nourished on the Gospel proclaimed at this service? As we carry out that wish, may the Spirit of God fill us with comfort, strength, and hope, so that we go forth from this service not bowed down with despair but enlightened from on high.

The meaning of the prayer, "Thy will be done," is found alone in Him who offered it and taught us so to pray. In the person, message, and work of Jesus Christ the will of God is revealed. Jesus said, "I have come down from heaven not to do My own will, but the will of Him who sent Me" (John 6:38). And again, "My food is to do the will of Him who sent me and to accomplish His work" (John 4:34). God would not have His will remain obscure. The work of His Son manifests the Father's will, the will of Him who "so loved the world that He gave His only Son, that whoever believes in Him should not perish but have eternal life." (John 3:16)

God's will means God Himself in action for us through Christ, His Son. To utter that prayer, them, is a battle cry of faith. It is an earnest appeal to God that He would call us to His side in the doing of His will on this earth, where His will meets opposition and must fight its way through. It is not an utterance of blind despair, as though now that everything else has been tried and failed, the will of God should at last be done! This is not the prayer of one who has given up, who folds his hands in resignation from life and the world and throws himself finally upon fate. No, Jesus Himself unfolds the meaning of this prayer as a cry of faith and a summons to action. In Gethsemane He prayed that the cup of suffering be taken from Him, but He added, "Not My will but Thine be done." This was God's answer, that the cup of suffering would pass only by His drinking it to the last bitter dregs. Jesus prayed, "Thy will be done," and then went to the cross. That is anything but passive resignation. That is the event in which the salvation of the world is fashioned by the Father. Because Jesus made His will one with the Father's, He was delivered into the hands of sinners and crucified. But God raised Him from the dead in power, and now He lives to shed on men's hearts the Holy Spirit, who enables us to pray from our hearts, "Thy will be done."

It is an unspeakably great miracle of divine grace that our own wayward and self-willed lives come under the sway of God's gracious will. Things happen in life when one can pray, not grudgingly or with reservations but wholeheartedly, "Thy will be done," for this prayer represents the victory of God's infinitely greater and wiser will over our own.

This is the key that unfolds the inner meaning of Otto Geiseman's life. Two instances stand out wherein the will of God prevailed over his own will. The first comes from his early years. As a lad of 13 he brought gladness to the hearts of his parents with his desire to prepare for the ministry. But when he went off to preparatory school, he encountered a cold formalism and a legalistic brand of Christianity that repelled him. Not a few times during his college years he would go off by himself under the stars and wrestle with God about this matter of serving in the ministry. He had finally reached the decision to enter another profession and serve out his life as a Christian layman removed from the angularities of little men entrusted with a great calling. But the sudden death by drowning of a classmate worked a change in his mind. As he stood over the body of his close friend, he asked himself why his life should be spared and his friend's taken. The determination to become a pastor returned to him and with it the realization that the will of God was that his life should be useful in changing the loveless atmosphere of a hardened orthodoxy into what orthodox Christian faith truly means: straight thinking about the love of God for sinners. The lives of all of us here today, and of many more not here, have been blessed because the will of God prevailed nearly a half-century ago in Pastor Geiseman's young life.

Another and more forceful instance of the prevailing of God's will is taken from the end of his life. Some 11 weeks ago, when he entered the hospital, he took with him a fervent will to live. His desire to recover and return to his loved ones and the calling that he loved to the depths of his being was not lukewarm. His heart was set on work yet to do. As the disease pressed in harder and harder upon him, the most fundamental battle of human existence raged within him. That battle is to pray from the heart, "Thy will be done," even when this prayer means saying good-bye to all that is dear to one on earth. Now this was the prayer on Pastor's lips constantly throughout this time of rugged temptation and struggle. Do not think that because one is a pastor there is no struggle with death! Nor should we think that this final ordeal of his last sickness is something totally incongruous and incompatible with the rest of his life of service to God and man. If we will look at life in this way, "Thy will be done," then this last chapter in Pastor's life is the greatest of all, for then it means the victory of heavenly over earthly hopes. Then it means the good and gracious will of God has been done, and the temporal has given way to the eternal. This is the great lesson God teaches through suffering, that when one's own will is broken through the bearing of the cross, it very often happens that the doing of God's will truly begins. God kills in order to bring to life. He leads men to crosses and suffering that the new man may rise to live in righteousness and purity forever. But only in Christ is this mystery unfolded. Only His Spirit can teach us this eternal good that God fashions out of what otherwise is utter hell on earth.

Between these two events that bracket Pastor's ministerial life lies this wonderful and remarkable record of what happens when a forgiven sinner prays from his heart, "Thy will be done." Look carefully now at his life, and understand it as the unfolding of the will of the Triune God in a most gracious manner. If we may see Pastor's life in this light, as an instrument of the will of the Holy Trinity, we may not only rejoice in God's goodness to Pastor Geiseman but take heart in the goodness of His will toward us as well.

Think of the delight Dr. Geiseman took in our heavenly Father's good world of such marvelous creation. Whether it was a fine spring day, a mellow glass of wine, a creative work of art, a skillfully placed golf shot, an able business-man or farmer, a lovely lady, a determined drummer in a band, or the graceful movements of a child dancing to a tune, Pastor had a way of seeing it as a part of God's good world. His eye was turned appreciatively toward excellence wherever he met it. Some might be puzzled over how a minister could take interest in so many "worldly" things. Others might misunderstand this in another way by simply calling him a born aristocrat. But neither view will do. What we have here is the result of praying from the heart, "Thy will be done on earth," and then realizing that God made the world for His children to relish and enjoy. This gave Pastor a point of contact with people from all walks of life who were distant from the Christian faith. Civic affairs, public welfare, the for-tunes of commerce and government, higher education, and so many other facets of the world's ongoing life held a fascination for him. Why? Because he sensed the Father's continuous work of creating and preserving and loving this remarkable world of His. Yet Pastor Geise-man harbored virtually no illusions about what happens when the world is made an end in itself. He lived too close to the tragedies that occur when men idolize the creation instead of worshiping the Creator.

Sin means putting something or someone other than God first in the heart. This demonic force turns spouse against spouse, splits parents and children in bitterness, pits employer against employee, teacher against pupil, and pastor against congregation. The one power that prevails over sin is the love of God revealed supremely in the cross of Christ. This goodness of the forgiveness of sins reaches men through the Gospel. The will of the Father above all else is this, that His redeeming love in His beloved Son be the center of life. There is no substitute for this center, and Pastor's life and ministry demonstrate what immense blessings issue from the changeless Gospel of God's transforming love for a world that turned its back on Him. In the power of the Gospel, pastor and people were held together throughout 40 years of ministry in Grace Church. In the power of the Gospel, people's varied gifts and backgrounds were brought into a harmonious spirit of unity. In the power of the Gospel, selfishness was changed into generosity and cynicism into faith. In the power of the Gospel, marriages were saved from oblivion, broken hearts were healed, drooping spirits were lifted, and despairing minds were given new vision. The freshness of God's love in Christ did not lose its luster in Pastor's ministry. This was because the Holy Spirit allowed him to apply it first to his own needs and then to the needs of so many. When we came to him with our heartaches or little vexations, we received more than sympathy, understanding, or good advice. In him we met the Christ. In him some new facet of the Savior's love was pointed out. In the pulpit, in the study, in hospitals, homes, jails, railroad cars, planes, boats, and sometimes in bars, Otto Geiseman held the cross before people as the one

source of new life in God. This above all endears his
memory to us, that through him we know better the God
of love and grace. This is what takes place when a man
prays from his heart, "Thy will be done on earth as it is
in heaven." Life is then centered in the Gospel.

When one prays sincerely that God's will be done, that
very prayer is the sign of the presence of the Holy Spirit
in the heart. He is the Lord and Giver of God's life to
those who know their need before the Father. Here is
where the will of God has been most powerfully fulfilled
in Pastor's life and work, his emphasis upon the Spirit
of God as the One who calls, gathers, enlightens, and
sanctifies the whole Christian church on earth and keeps
it with Jesus Christ in the true faith. This gives the Christian a clear view of himself, his congregation, and his
church denomination. Pastor knew that all three were
fallible, human, and in need of daily forgiveness. His
courage to speak out against those who felt that the Holy
Spirit worked chiefly among Lutherans did not always
make him popular. But this has been the price paid by
all the Lord's servants who put the Spirit over the letter,
the Gospel over the Law, and the glory of God over the
pride of men. Also it is the reason why a considerable
amount of church history gathers around men of the Spirit
who can pray, "Thy will be done," and then let the chips
fall where they may.

There is another great truth connected with the Spirit's
work. It is the gift of creativity. The Holy Spirit is out
ahead of the organized Christian movement, beckoning
to us through men of vision and creative minds to follow
Him. The creativity does not consist in inventing a new

Gospel. It lies in applying creatively the Gospel to every realm of life. Here is where the Spirit of God was so good to our Pastor. It did not matter what the proposal was, the question he would ask sounded like this: "Are we merely making a gesture or are we devoting our creative best to following the lead of the Spirit?" This point of view made him invaluable in the first work of his life, the parish ministry. But beyond that it also contributed positively to the decisions of boards and committees charged with the larger responsibilities of the church. In planning a church dinner or in planning a church building such as this one, there was a consistent care to do it creatively. Anything done for God must be done with the best we have. This gift of the Spirit was contagious; it inspired him to evoke in others the will to do their utmost for God. This is one more convincing evidence of what takes place when God's will is done on earth as it is in heaven: His Holy Spirit leads men on to creative vision and work.

Many, many more things could be said about God's will at work in Pastor's life. Each of us can turn back in his memory to incidents and events in which he has been Christ's faithful shepherd to us. Let us see them all in the light of the Triune God bringing His will to be done on earth as it is in heaven. Our abiding hope and true comfort is that the Triune God, who opens men's eyes to His good world, leads them to cherish His redeeming love in Christ, His Son, and empowers them by His Holy Spirit to a life of creative service, does not abandon His children or His church. He has brought the victory and peace of Christ to this servant of His, and that is why we sing Easter music of praise today. And that is why we, who face a new future, can pray confidently this prayer that spans all our needs and joins heaven with earth:

> Thy will be done by us on earth,
> Even as it is done by those who are in heaven.

Into Thy Hand I Commit My Spirit
(for a pastor)

Psalm 31:5   Arno C. Scholz

It is strange, isn't it, that we should speak of a little infant as being old? We say that it is a day old, a week old, a month old. By this very expression we are subscribing to the solemn truth that we begin to die the very moment we are born. Our life on this earth is but a journey to the grave. In the Bible we are told, "Sin came into the world through one man and death through sin" (Rom. 5:12). Whether one lives but a few days or more than fourscore years, his life finally ends in a grave. There are no exceptions. "It is appointed for men to die once" (Heb. 9:27). At the appointed time all lie down and die. No man and no angel can save us from death and the grave. Death came into the world by sin, "and so death spread to all men because all men sinned." (Rom. 5:12)

But that doesn't mean that we must stand in hopeless grief around the caskets of our believing loved ones. Not at all. We have a message of comfort for the children of the departed one, the sons and daughters whom he fondly cherished; we have comfort for the many friends who mourn his departure. When our believing loved ones are taken from us by death, when they are separated from all they hold dear in this world, we have more than pleasant memories of what they meant to us in this life. We have the positive assurance that all who die in the Lord are blessed in the world beyond the grave, that they have passed from death to life, and that they await our arrival at the gates of Paradise, where all Christians will be reunited, never again to be parted.

No wonder, then, that the apostle Paul tells us that Christians do not shed tears of hopeless grief at the graves of their loved ones but comfort themselves with the certain hope that they will meet their departed ones before the throne of God in heaven, where they will join in singing praises to the Lamb who has redeemed them to God by His blood forever and ever.

You have lost a kind father; our congregation has lost a faithful and esteemed member; the church has lost a conscientious preacher of the Gospel; I personally have lost a true friend. All of us who were acquainted with Pastor Kohlmeier knew him as a humble child of God, a gentle soul, a sincere Christian, a faithful pastor, a quiet, unassuming disciple and follower of Jesus. He had long been at peace with God through our Lord Jesus Christ. Though he did not know when the angel of death would come for him, he was nevertheless aware that the end could not be far off, and he lived in daily expectation of the summons that would call him out of time into eternity. It was more than a year ago that he chose his own funeral text, the text to which I now direct your attention: "Into Thy hand I commit my spirit; Thou hast redeemed me, O Lord, faithful God."

These words are often quoted as if they are appropriate only for the final hours of life, when death is near. And it is true, Jesus Himself used them as His last words from the cross. They are fitting words for any dying believer. The first Christian martyr, Stephen, used them

as the stones were crushing out his life. He said, "Lord
Jesus, receive my spirit" (Acts 7:59). Martin Luther
twice spoke these words in his last hours. On the evening before he died, when he realized that the end was
close at hand, he prayed the very words of our text.
A few hours later and only moments before he breathed
his last, he prayed, "Father, into Thy hands I commend
my spirit. Thou hast redeemed me, Thou faithful God."
Then he died. That is the way to die.

But that is also the way to live. When David spoke
the words of our text, he was not thinking about his
death. He was in a great deal of trouble, surrounded by
all sorts of difficulties, confronted by innumerable problems. He was looking for help in the face of these difficulties and dangers. And so, too, our departed brother
did not wait until death was near to say, "Into Thy hand
I commit my spirit." He had made that confession many,
many years ago.

These words, "Into Thy hand I commit my spirit,"
imply that we submit ourselves wholly and completely to
God's will. This commitment is required of all those
who profess to be God's people. The moment we are
brought to faith in Christ we are moved to commit ourselves, body and soul, for time and for eternity, into the
keeping of the Lord Jesus Christ. We are to trust Him
fully and completely for everything in this life and in the
life which is to come.

Jesus taught us this same truth. He told us never to
worry about anything. He directed our attention to the
lilies and the birds and He reminded us that if our heavenly Father cares for the birds and clothes the flowers of

the field, He will much more care for and clothe us, His children.

Our departed brother not only talked this way; he also lived this way. And that accounts for the fact that he was always composed and serene. When on the occasion of his 80th birthday he was asked in a radio interview to what he ascribed his long life and cheerful disposition, he replied: "I have always tried to practice what I preached to my members: 'Cast all your cares upon Him, for He cares for you.'" Pastor Kohlmeier was never anxious about the morrow; he lived a day at a time with complete confidence in the gracious care and keeping of his heavenly Father. He was positive that Jesus was his Friend who had accepted him as His pardoned and forgiven child, One who would now guard and guide him through all the varied experiences of life, bringing him at last to heaven's gate.

That faith is expressed in the words, "Thou hast redeemed me." Pastor Kohlmeier looked to Jesus and saw in Him the Lamb of God that takes away the sin of the world. In the "despised and rejected of men" (Is. 53:3) he saw his Savior. Justified by faith, he had peace with God through our Lord Jesus Christ. To him the Savior had also bequeathed His peace, saying, "Peace I leave with you; My peace I give to you" (John 14:27). No one who knew our departed brother could help but know that here was a man whose heart was at ease. When the hour of his departure drew near, he willingly bade farewell to this world of sin and suffering and walked peacefully through the valley of the shadow of death until he came to his inheritance "imperishable, undefiled, and unfading." (1 Peter 1:4)

"Thou hast redeemed me" — this faith was implanted in the heart of our brother in early infancy in the Sacrament of Holy Baptism, and this was his faith to the very end. Later on when God had so guided and directed his life that our brother was moved to prepare himself for the holy ministry, this was the theme of all his preaching. That's the message he proclaimed for more than 50 years, and that was his confession even to the end: "I believe that Jesus Christ is my Lord, who has redeemed me." So he lived, and so he died.

Through death your father has now entered into his eternal rest. As he had committed himself to Christ for life, so also did he trust Him as the hour of death drew near. As he had lived unto the Lord, so he also died unto the Lord, trusting not in his own merit or worthiness but in the redemption Christ purchased for him. Let that be your comfort and consolation.

What's more, we haven't really been separated from him; we remain united to him in spite of death. Christ is the Lord both of the living and the dead. All the children of God here on earth and yonder in heaven are one blessed family, members of Christ's body, and therefore intimately bound together. There is only this difference: we are still living on the earth, while those who have fallen asleep in Jesus are already safely home; we who remain behind see the glory of heaven only as "through a glass darkly," but our departed loved ones "face to face." (1 Cor. 13:12)

Therefore we will comfort ourselves as we stand here in the presence of death. Our departed brother in Christ has entered the more abundant life and now sings praises to the Savior together with the angels and all the host of the redeemed. And may you, the sons and daughters of the departed, today dedicate yourselves anew to the service of Christ, to go forth to build in the Savior's name a higher and nobler monument than one of stone to mark your father's earthly resting place, namely the monument of truly Christian lives, for which he laid the foundation when he baptized, instructed, and confirmed you. And may this also be your daily confession and prayer, now in the days of health and strength as well as in the hour of death, "Into Thy hand I commit my spirit; Thou hast redeemed me, O Lord, faithful God."

An Inspired Eulogy for a Great Man of God
(for a church official)

2 Kings 2:12   W. Harry Krieger

When on Monday last at 2:20 o'clock a telephone call
brought the sad news of the sudden death of our beloved
Dr. Andrew Zeile, the lamentation of the prophet Elisha
came swiftly to mind. His teacher Elijah had been removed from earth to heaven, suddenly, mysteriously.
"And Elisha saw it, and he cried: 'My father, my father,
the chariots of Israel and its horsemen!' "

This cry is drenched with tears; it expresses a sorrow
too deep for words and too painful for utterance. When
today we force ourselves to the thought that we shall
see Dr. Zeile no more on earth, that his steadying voice
will no more be heard, that his presence will be here no
longer to bless us, then we look up from the shadowy
depths of bereavement and cry: "My father, my father,
the chariots of Israel and its horsemen!"

But these words of Holy Writ are much more than the
heart's lament in the midst of loss. They are in essence
and in their original setting an inspired eulogy for a
great man of God. I have therefore chosen them as
the funeral text for the one whose passing we mourn
together.

Were it your funeral service or mine, these words
would scarcely be fitting. But as we pause to reflect
on the life and labors of this father in God, we know in

our hearts that the text applies. When we think of his life — so willing in its surrender to Christ, so rich in its achievements for the church, so abundant in its service to multitudes — we find this life epitomized and properly evaluated in this single memorable sentence: "My father, my father, the chariots of Israel and its horsemen!"

These words were originally spoken of a great man of God in the Old Testament — the prophet Elijah. We cannot go on to add that these words were his funeral text, for that would not be accurate. For Elijah there was no funeral service and no burial — only the beckoning hand of a faithful God at the close of his life and then the chariot of fire and the whirlwind which carried him aloft to heaven. Like Enoch before him, he was translated that he should not see death: "And he was not, for God took him." (Gen. 5:24)

On the coming Sunday the church is called to observe the Feast of the Transfiguration of our Lord. Of all the heroes of the Old Testament, the two who were chosen to appear in glory on the holy mount and to speak with Jesus concerning His approaching death at Jerusalem as the Sinbearer and Substitute for us poor sinners — of them all, the two who were chosen were Moses and *Elijah*. If on this occasion our Lord found it profitable to speak with Elijah, it will not be without profit for us to look for a while at this unusual figure. For us to review briefly the prophetic ministry of Elijah is to appreciate more fully the life and ministry of Andrew Zeile and, what is more important, to see the grace and greatness of God as they were manifested in him.

Elijah, like John the Baptist, is one of the greatest men of the Bible, and one of the loneliest. He appeared on the stage of Israel's history like a meteor in the midnight sky. It was a time of national apostasy when a wicked king had led Israel down the dark and evil path of idolatry. So bad had the situation in the life of the Old Testament church become that Elijah came for a while to believe that he was the only one left who had remained faithful to God. At such a perilous time God called this man to stand in the gap before Him for the land, that He should not destroy it. On page after page of the Old Testament his career unfolds. Elijah is ever the uncompromising reformer, insisting on whole-souled service to God and condemning divided allegiance. He meets and conquers at Carmel the priests and prophets of Baal; he overthrows the rampant idolatries of his day; he defies Ahab and his iniquitous Queen Jezebel; and by the sheer force of his spirituality, which had its roots deep in the Word of God, he repairs the gap in the walls of the Old Testament church and holds the nation together. Oh, to be sure, the prophet Elijah experienced his share of disappointments. He passed through many a fierce ordeal, and great trial was made of his faith. Most memorable, perhaps, was the time he fled before the burning chariot of Jezebel's wrath, fled for his very life. Into the desert he fled, utterly discouraged because all his work seemed in vain and all his ministry futile and profitless. Falling down beneath a juniper tree at length, he cried out to God: "It is enough; now, O Lord, take away my life, for I am no better than my fathers" (1 Kings 19:4). But his despondency lasts for only a little while. Elijah is restored by a new vision of God and by new assignments that bring larger responsibilities. There are kings to anoint and a successor to be chosen; there are seminaries, the "schools of the prophets," to found, and there are young laborers for the Lord to counsel and strengthen. And always, always there are the multitudes of God's people to tend and to shepherd. For Elijah there is no retirement. He is active to the last, to that wonderful day when he is led to the banks of the Jordan and the familiar Voice whispers, "Come, Elijah, it is time for you to make the crossing and to enter into rest."

In the life and ministry of Andrew Zeile we have one who went before the Lord "in the spirit and power of Elijah."

What a blessing God made him to be for the members of Bethlehem Congregation! For almost 45 years he served you faithfully as shepherd and spiritual leader. His enduring love for the people of this parish was as genuine as it was beautiful to see. Despite the high office and the honors that came to him in later life, Bethlehem Congregation remained his "first love." For Andrew Zeile there was no higher calling than that of parish pastor. Where his sermons were concerned, he was bound by the mandate of Dr. Luther, who declared: "One thing you must preach: The wisdom of the cross!" For almost a half-century he pointed you to the Lamb of God that takes away the sins of the world. His one great concern was to strengthen you in this holy faith, the faith that looks to Jesus Christ alone as Savior and Lord. The secret and source of his power as a preacher are to be found in his loyalty to God's Book, his trust in the precious blood, and his confident assurance of the blessed hope which is ours as the people of Christ. For 45 years he brought to the members of this congregation comfort in sorrow, strength in weakness, and courage in adversity.

Now suddenly he is taken from you and sorrow fills your hearts. In remembrance of all that he has meant to Bethlehem Church, there is not a member, young or old, who does not say: "My father, my father, the chariots of Israel and its horsemen!" But God calls you to do more than to weep and mourn. In this solemn hour God summons you to remember the Word which the departed preached to you, that it may continue to bring forth fruit in your lives. Through this Word He will bring you comfort and assurance and at the last also make you victorious.

"The chariots of Israel and its horsemen!" Surely these words sum up Dr. Zeile's significance for the larger kingdom. In losing him, this District has lost a great champion of the faith, an ardent churchman, a wise and resourceful leader in the army of Jesus Christ. With keen insight and following long observation, Dr. Luther once asserted: "The ambitious preacher is a pestilence to the church." Andrew Zeile was not ambitious for self but ambitious for God — and the Lord made him an ornament and a blessing to His church. Ever a humble man, he was perhaps unaware that God had set him apart as a chosen vessel and that he was being readied for a great responsibility. As financial secretary of the District for almost two decades, he became acquainted with congregations throughout the state, acquainted also with the broad scope of the District's work, and familiar with its complex problems and thrilling opportunities. Recognizing his exceptional gifts and deep consecration, the delegates to the convention in 1942 elected Dr. Zeile to the presidency of the District. He brought to this high office vast experience, high dedication, an endearing hu-

mility, a becoming dignity, and above all, a personal
faith beautiful both in its greatness and in its simplicity.

Here, then, was a servant of God able to inspire pastors
and people alike by the power of his personal example!
The 15 years of his presidency were marked by great
missionary conquests in this lower peninsula of Michigan.
Under his stirring leadership the number of Lutheran
Christians grew from 76,000 to 119,000. His influence
extended far beyond this state, however, for God made
him a blessing to all of Synod. He became the trusted
confidant of Synod's president and his wise counsel,
especially in financial affairs, was eagerly sought and always respected. To the very last his zeal for the welfare
of the church never flagged. Just a week before his
death he was present at an important conference of our
District and participated in the discussions with char-
acteristic vigor. Today, as the pastors of the District
take reluctant leave of him in submission to God's will,
the heart of each cries out: "My father, my father, the
chariots of Israel and its horsemen!"

Those who feel his loss most keenly are his beloved
wife and children and all who are bound to him by the
close ties of blood and kinship. The Lord in His great
goodness brought to Dr. Zeile's side a loyal and devoted
helpmeet to share his joys and sorrows. She knew all
his failings, found them to be few, and loved him still,
bringing into his life "beauty for ashes" and the "oil
of joy for heaviness of spirit." Their home was blessed
with the precious gift of children who patterned their
lives after the example of devout parents and who continue to bring honor to an honored name. What a joy
it was for Dr. Zeile to see his sons and his daughters

enter the service of the church as pastors or pastors' wives. For you, his children, this separation is painful. All the grief of your hearts and all the love you bear him is caught and held in the single word — father. "My father, my father!" Saying that word, you have no need to say more.

Is there now comfort for you and for us and for all who remain? We have reviewed the life and career of one whose ministry in our generation was much like that of God's prophet Elijah. But what happened to each at the end of it all, at the close of life?

For Elijah of old, the end was triumphant and glorious. What a convoy his Lord sent for him — "a chariot of fire," not for burning but for brightness, not to torture or consume him but to render his journey homeward conspicuous and illustrious. "And Elijah went up by a whirlwind into heaven." All the while Elisha stands by and looks on like one in a dream. Then, recovering himself, and gazing after his beloved leader's vanishing form, he cries: "My father, my father, the chariots of Israel and its horsemen!" But he soon resigns himself to God's will. He is comforted in the knowledge that Elijah has entered the glory everlasting, and he carries on the great work.

For our beloved father in God the close of life was also triumphant and glorious. The Lord he loved and served had fulfilled the promise: "Lo, I am with you always, to the close of the age" (Matt. 28:20). Dr. Zeile looked forward with rejoicing to the day when the Lord would call him home. The thought of death left him undismayed and unafraid. Like Luther and many a saint of God, he had grown "homesick for heaven." He was sure of the love of Christ, certain that his sins, too, had been cleansed in the precious blood. He knew the One he was to meet. Suddenly, on Monday last, the Lord called, and his soul took its flight heavenward, on into the glorious presence of the King! For him —

> The strife is o'er, the battle done;
> Now is the Victor's triumph won;
> Now be the song of praise begun. *TLH* 210:1

We thank and praise God for His marvelous grace and mercy which He showed unto His servant. We shall go forward, trusting His promise to raise us at the Last Day and reunite us with those who have gone before. And we shall leave His house this day with the fervent prayer: "Let me die the death of the righteous, and let my last end be like his." Let me live as Elijah lived and as Thy servant Andrew lived, and so shall I — even though I pass through the valley of the shadow of death — enter as did they into the Father's house of many mansions, the home eternal in the heavens, the blessed "with Me" of Jesus, my faithful God and Savior. "Hear my prayer, O Lord; let my cry come to Thee!" (Ps. 102:1)

Everything Has Become Fresh and New
(memorial for a youth counselor)

2 Corinthians 5:14-17   Elmer N. Witt

The story of God's man is the story of God.

We are gathered in this church because of God. We are able in these moments of meditation to speak calmly and directly about death, because of God. We are unafraid to talk about Chief, about his life, his work, and his death, not in sentimentality, but because of God.

Many religious people tell us to accept death as a natural thing. Perhaps they mean that it is inevitable. But it is not natural. We are not created to die. We can say "man is born to die" only because of what went wrong with God's plans, God's will. The death of man is an unnatural thing. It points to the ultimate disorder in ourselves and in the world around us. It is God's judgment on man gone wrong, on man turned aside from his Creator.

For this reason Christians do not pretend to understand death any more than they can understand life. This is why Christians say "We believe" rather than "We have the answer." We believe there has been a break-through in the distortion, the disruption and the despair of this judgment of God which is death. This break-through is nothing less than God Himself.

For it is Christ, the visible expression of the invisible God, who gives us life from the dead, because He Himself took death into His own body. And because of Him, death is dead. Because of Him, resurrection from death is not merely a live option; it's an accomplished fact.

The apostle Paul declares in our text that everything has become fresh and new.

I believe this is true about Chief Weiherman, not only now in the obviousness of death but perhaps even more in the swiftness of life. Everything became fresh and new in the days of Chief because of what God made him, because of what God accomplished in his 68 years, 8 months, and 21 days upon earth.

Our knowledge of Chief is not based on his outward life. He was ordinary in many ways, viewed from this perspective. There are likely many like him who have lived and are living now. But we view Chief as he is in Christ. He was extraordinary, and we knew and saw it, because of Christ. That's why we can say without hesitation that to speak of him is to speak of God. For as surely as God was in Christ, so surely was Christ in Chief and Chief in God.

The start of his "life together" with God was at a baptismal font in Hinckley, Ill., in the name of the Father and of the Son and of the Holy Ghost.

This new life with God is going on now, perfectly, gloriously since our Lord took Chief last Sunday. All this is God's doing, for He has reconciled us all to Himself in Christ Jesus, not counting our sins against us, continually cleansing us from the past and continually giving us power for what lies ahead.

This is what we saw in Chief Weiherman in his days among us. The outstanding dimension of his life ministry is that God enabled him to serve so many people directly.

Chief was not an evangelist in the usual sense of this word. Rather, Chief saw the whole of his life, his calling and work, as the love of God in action. As schoolroom teacher, youth leader, camp manager, counselor of theologians, father, friend and husband . . . the difference with Chief was that "everything had become fresh and new." He was wont to say a thousand times, "Christianity is not a way to do certain things but a certain way of doing everything."

So Chief loved the world, not in a selfish way, of course, but in God's way. He loved the world of people in which God had placed him. His gregariousness and warm handshake were symbols of this love.

Chief loved nature. Many of us who explored life with him at Camp Arcadia will never view trees or flowers or stars the same way again because of Chief, who saw everything fresh and new.

Chief loved humor. It relieved tense moments. It relaxed tired minds. In conversation or at a banquet, it made things fresh and new.

Chief loved travel. He saw God's love expressed in Europe, South America, Central America, and in every state and province.

And Chief loved progress. In the very board meeting that was crowned with his death, Chief contributed again and again with positive, forward-looking views. He was always the youngest person in any group. "The road to success is always under construction," he said, and he believed he was part of the construction crew of God in the business of making everything fresh and new.

If a man is in Christ! We have said that Chief was in Christ, but this was not perfectly true. It is true of no person upon earth. Chief Weiherman had his faults, his failings, his inconsistencies. Possibly those closest to him saw these best and often loved him because of them. We are continually in the process of becoming fresh and new. This is why God's mercies are new to us every morning, why the water in Holy Baptism reminds us at the start of each day that the old person in us must drown and die and a new man, God's man, must arise and live.

God does not restore His image perfectly this side of the grave. As Prof. Richard Caemmerer illustrates in *God's Great Plan for You,* his book dedicated to Mom and Chief:

> [St. Paul] says that God's man, and particularly God's servant who speaks the Word for Him, may suffer difficulty and fatigue, but he constantly undergoes repair and improvement. He is helped more fully to display the image of God as he himself gazes into the "glory of God," namely, God's own display to him of His love and power in the work of Jesus Christ completed on the cross and sealed in the resurrection on Easter morning.
>
> This life of drawing on the goodness of God in Christ goes on in the secret of our minds, whenever we are pondering Christ's work for us. But it also is the pursuit of God's people as they gather together and remind one another of Christ's work and God's provision for them. They do this as they speak to one another in their households and families; as they worship together and sing their psalms and hymns to one another; as they remind one another in their gatherings that Jesus Christ is the Great High Priest who cleared the road to God for them. This the Bible calls "letting the Word of Christ dwell in us richly." It is not merely an exercise in thinking of Christ and the Cross, but it is the power by which Chris-

tians are then enabled to carry out the program that
God has for them when He puts them into His image.

This is what we have seen and heard in the life of Chief
Weiherman. And to this we testify, that he is in Christ.
And we thank and praise God for this freshness and
newness of life.

And this indeed is Chief's final message to us, even in
his departure. As an ambassador for Christ he urges us,
"Make your peace with God!" The suddenness of his
death reminds us that we are all apostles of urgency,
evangelists of the final hour. "Now is the acceptable time;
behold, now is the day of salvation." (2 Cor. 6:2)

The past is finished and gone for us too. With His
love God has wiped clean the slate of our sins, our for-
getting of His mercy, our failure to be what He has made
us in Christ. In His only-begotten Son He has made the
new Covenant with us and sealed it in the death of our
Lord and Savior. He has given us the *new* Spirit, whom
Peter describes as bringing "seasons of refreshing from
the presence of the Lord." The very peace of God we
proclaim is *new;* it is the *Good News.* And that is why
religious truth always strikes us fresh and is always *news,*
no matter how often we have previously heard or experienced it.

And God will make *new* heavens and a *new* earth, and
a *new* Jerusalem will be established, which Chief now
knows but for which we patiently wait the restoration
of all things.

Every day we experience something of death of the
Lord Jesus so that we may also know the power of the
life of Jesus in these bodies of ours. We are always

facing death, but this means that we know more and more of life. We speak because we believe, and we know for certain that He who raised the Lord Jesus from death shall also by Him raise us. We are children of the resurrection.

For if a man is in Christ, he becomes a new person altogether — the past is finished and gone, everything has become fresh and new.

Those of us who were with Chief this past weekend at Arcadia know this in a special way. At the end of this meeting of fellowship in the Gospel and in the joy of ministering to youth, our worship focused on the resurrection of Christ and His saints. We sang aloud the confident hymn, "Christ the Lord is risen again, Christ has broken death's strong chain."

As we worshiped, Chief was in another room close by and, unknown to us, on the threshold of that fresh and new day. Now we know that as we joined in the explanation of the Second Article of the Creed, we were saying this for and with Chief,

> that Jesus Christ, true God, begotten of the Father from eternity, and also true man, born of the Virgin Mary, is my Lord, who has redeemed me, a lost and condemned creature, purchased and won me from all sins, from death, and from the power of the devil; not with gold or silver, but with His holy, precious blood and with His innocent suffering and death, that I may be His own and live under Him in His kingdom and serve Him in everlasting righteousness, innocence, and blessedness, even as He is risen from the dead, lives and reigns to all eternity. This is most certainly true.

Chief and Christ live eternally — everything is fresh and new. Amen. This is most certainly true. Amen.